The Visions of the Pylons

*A Magical Record of Exploration
in the Starry Abode*

The Magician.
by Robert Buratti.

The Visions of the Pylons

A Magical Record of Exploration in the Starry Abode

August 22, 1975 E.V.
to February 5, 1977 E.V.

J. Daniel Gunther

Ibis Press
Lake Worth, Florida

Published in 2018 by Ibis Press
A division of Nicolas-Hays, Inc.
P. O. Box 540206
Lake Worth, FL 33454-0206
www.ibispress.net

Distributed to the trade by
Red Wheel/Weiser, LLC
65 Parker St. • Ste. 7
Newburyport, MA 01950
www.redwheelweiser.com

Copyright © 2018 by J. Daniel Gunther

All rights reserved.
No part of this publication may be reproduced or transmitted in any form or by any means, electronic or mechanical, including photocopying, recording, or by any information storage and retrieval system, without permission in writing from Nicolas-Hays, Inc. Reviewers may quote brief passages.

ISBN: 978-0-89254-183-6
Ebook ISBN: 978-0-89254-676-3

Library of Congress Cataloging-in-Publication Data
Available upon request

Book design and production by STUDIO 31
www.studio31.com

Jacket painting by NANCY WASSERMAN

Photo of painting by STUART PHOTOGRAPHY COMPANY

Printed in the United States of America
[MP]

Contents

Preface by Frater ΦANHΣ 7

Introduction 13

Pylon One: *Zemyeta* 31

Pylon Two: *Sepedeta-wawau* 41

Pylon Three: *Nebeta-za-tzefu* 57

Pylon Four: *Eiry-ta* 69

Pylon Five: *Nebeta-aḥau* 83

Pylon Five (Second Skry): *Nebeta-aḥau* 97

Pylon Six: *Ḥemut-neb-es* 107

Pylon Six (Second Skry): *Ḥemut-neb-es* 115

Pylon Seven: *Pezedey-ta* 127

Appendix One: 141
    The Names of the Pylons, their Attributions
    and their Guardians

Appendix Two: 145
    The Sigils of the Serpent Ones who are the
    Guardians of the Pylons

Appendix Three: 155
    The Images to be Engraved upon the Waxen Seals

Appendix Four: How to Skry the Pylons 169

APPENDIX FIVE:	177

    Of the Eucharist, being the Saffron Cakes,
        Milk and Honey

APPENDIX SIX:	181

    The Signs of Banishing and Invoking for the Pylons

BIBLIOGRAPHY	187
INDEX	195

COLOR INSERT (follows page 144)

    The Reflections of the Sephiroth and Paths in the Pylons
    Angelic Sigil of Fire
    The Pantacle of *Zooωasar*

Preface

Do what thou wilt shall be the whole of the Law.

In 1909 e.v., the Prophet of Thelema, Aleister Crowley, began to publish *The Equinox*, the official organ of A∴A∴, the teaching Order which he administered. In this seminal periodical, the editor started to expound upon a revolutionary method of enlightenment he labeled Scientific Illuminism. Soon, *The Equinox* would come to include accounts of spiritual practices and even diary materials from both Crowley and his pupils. The tradition continues to this day.[1] The intent is clear: to share the result of some of the practices of the System of the A∴A∴ published in *The Equinox*, and to make the experiments open to external scrutiny and peer review.

In the method of Scientific Illuminism, a broad discipline surrounds the recording procedures so as to further help the Student integrate the experience; also, in the case of visionary practices, to separate the wheat from the chaff, the genuine transpersonal experiences from the simple byproducts deriving from the Aspirant's psychology. *The Visions of the Pylons* continues in this long-established tradition of recorded magical works.

The operation documented here uses as its basis a central funerary Egyptian text, the so-called *Book of Pylons* (or *Gates*). It refers to the nocturnal journey of the deceased on the Solar Bark in the Starry Abode. There he actively participates in the regenerative process that leads to sunrise; and in his own personal ascension he will take part in the cosmic balance.

---

1 *The Equinox*, Volumes I, III and IV.

The text was chosen to specifically explore the Egyptian plane.² In order to ensure spiritual coherence, the names of the Pylons and their Guardians contained in the original text were selected and transformed into working formulæ. Magical techniques and ceremonial procedures were then devised to access and explore the astral plane. Eventually, these were enlarged and refined for future exploration. Sigils and talismans were extracted and eucharistic techniques introduced to the procedure. These can best be retraced in the Curriculum³ established for the Grades of the Outer College of A∴A∴ that lead to Adeptship. After all, the Curriculum was also designed to enable the Student to access and tackle archetypal data while exploring subtler planes of reality.

I was first introduced to *The Visions of the Pylons* in September 2017 E.V., while co-lecturing with Brother Daniel in Austin, Texas. Jet-lagged as I was, the first thing I perceived was the magical creativity underlying the preparatory work itself. The way in which source material over thirty-five centuries old⁴ was being experimentally handled was fascinating; on the other hand, the methodology applied was obviously in harmony with the magical and mystical system of the A∴A∴ in which the author had been trained.

The text quoted during the lecture appeared very intimate, and attuned to the author's personal devotion to the Egyptian Goddess Maat. But the actual content started to unmistakably resonate with my own cryptoglyphs. What surprised me even more was the discovery that the intelligences involved in the

---

[2] See "Notes for an Astral Atlas" in A. Crowley, M. Desti, and L. Waddell, *Magick. Book 4, Parts I–IV*, ed. Hymenaeus Beta (2nd rev. ed., York Beach, Maine: Samuel Weiser, 1997), Appendix III.

[3] See "A∴A∴ Curriculum" in Crowley, *op. cit.*, Appendix I.

[4] The last known and most complete version of *The Book of Pylons* was engraved in a Theban tomb at the beginning of the 26th Dynasty (7th century B.C.E.).

Visions were not only aware of the Law of Thelema, but that the very Guardians of the Pylons seemed to have accepted it. Another example of this phenomenon in Thelemic writings may be found in *The Vision and the Voice*.[5]

This work offers an example of the application of the entire Outer College modus operandi, filtered through the perspective of the A∴A∴ Grade the author held at the time. It is therefore a welcome addition to the Order's literature, and warrants consideration in terms of the Task[6] of Philosophus 4°= 7□. The next Grade in the A∴A∴ System, that of Dominus Liminis, can only be granted by Authority. On the stable roof of Destruction, his or her Mastery will be disputed until the Aspirant comes to forge a more exalted link to the chain of Adepts. In the original Egyptian book, the blessed dead is only admitted to the Hall of Judgment after his heart is weighed and found void of falsehood—and thus in perfect balance with Truth. While the plummet is identified with the Egyptian God Thoth, the empty scale indicates that the heart has been replaced by the invisible Eye of Horus.

Incidentally, the appearance in some Visions of formulas pertaining to the Hieros Gamos adumbrate part of the Task[7] of another fiery Grade, that of Adeptus Major 6°= 5□. The beings encountered summoned the Seer to open the Mysteries of Creation.

The notes to the text also provide important perspective on the work of the Adept. For the knowledge gained by experience,

---

[5] A. Crowley, V. Neuburg and M. Desti, *The Vision and the Voice with Commentary and Other Papers The Equinox* IV(2), ed. Hymenaeus Beta (York Beach, Maine: Samuel Weiser, 1998).

[6] See "Liber 185" in A. Crowley, H.P. Blavatsky, J.F.C. Fuller and C.S. Jones, *Commentaries on the Holy Books and Other Papers, The Equinox* IV(2), ed. Hymenaeus Beta (York Beach, Maine: Samuel Weiser, 1996).

[7] See "One Star in Sight" in Crowley, *Magick*, Appendix II, part IX. Cf. *The Vision and the Voice, with Commentary and Other Papers*.

structured and organized, will then be used against itself, so as to radically challenge both conscious apperception and instinctive apprehension. This is an integral part of the preparatory toil leading to the next great crisis of the A∴A∴ system, the Ordeal of the Abyss.

As is often the case with truly magical books, there is a lot of wit between the lines. The Seer and the Scribe are engaged in the agelong battle of Man to understand, no matter the price. Ultimately, this is a book about freedom. For this, I am grateful that others convinced the author to share this gem with us.

In the small Egyptian museum in my hometown is preserved a polychrome relief from the tomb of Pharaoh Sety I, on whose sarcophagus was reproduced one of the best preserved versions of the Egyptian *Book of Pylons*. This beautifully colored relief shows the Lady of the West, Hathor, giving her necklace to the Pharaoh while holding his hand—a token of Her Love. The Pharaoh is depicted with sandals on his feet, robed in the veil of Glory, girdled with the multicolored pendant of Horus the Behdetite, and crowned with the royal Uraeus serpent. There is no part of him that is not of the Gods.

The present tome and its voluminous appendices invite the prepared seeker to further explore the Pylons. The Guardians clearly expect this. For some of them, Two Thousands Years is as One Day.

Amore è la legge, amore sotto la volontà.

Fraternally,

Fr. ΦΑΝΗΣ X°
National Grand Master General
Ordo Templi Orientis
Grand Lodge of Italy

The goddess Hathor, Lady of the West, giving her necklace to Pharaoh Sety I—from the ancient Egyptian Book of Pylons.

Plate LVIII, in I. Rosellini, *I monumenti dell'Egitto e della Nubia. Parte II: Monumenti civili, Tomo I* (Pisa: Niccolò Capurro, 1834).

Introduction

Do what thou wilt shall be the whole of the Law.

This is the Record of a series of Magical Workings by two young Magicians (we were both in our mid-twenties) seeking to deepen our understanding of the Magical Universe. The Visions documented herein are the results of an experiment we conducted between August 22, 1975 e.v. and February 5, 1977 e.v., whose purpose was to explore the Pylons of the *Duant*, or "Starry Abode."[1]

From the very beginning of Egyptian history, people believed that the gods and goddesses—and men and women—were all subject to the same laws of nature; they lived, grew old and died. A representation of this belief may be found in *The Book of the Heavenly Cow*, which recounts the rebellion of mankind against Ra because he had grown old and feeble.[2]

In time, the ancient Egyptians came to believe that only the bodies died; spirits were eternal. For example, the legend of the death of the god Osiris at the hands of the treacherous Set is

---

[1] I have chosen to follow the orthography of *Liber LXV*, II:2, rendering the Egyptian word ★𓅓𓂝𓏏, as *dw3t* "Duant," rather than the popular transliterations "Duat" or "Tuat." (Since *Liber LXV* is in Class A it is considered the final Authority in such matters.) Throughout the Visions, there are numerous occurrences of Egyptian god names. The transcription of these names may sometimes appear unusual, however they are merely an attempt to give the closest approximation I could make to the actual sound of the name heard. When known, the name of the god is given in the footnotes following the conventions of modern Egyptology.

[2] Cf. *The Angel and the Abyss*, pp. 25–28, for further discussion of this myth.

well known. His eternal spirit was resurrected by his wife Isis, and assisted by his son Horus, Osiris mounted unto the afterlife where he would reign as lord of the dead, personifying rebirth and life after death. Thus, they provided a place for their dead gods, and eventually, dead human beings as well. From the most primitive times, regardless of how it was conceived or visualized, it was called the *Duant*.

The concept of the *Duant* was vitally important to the ancient Egyptians. They visualized the world of the living as a place—between the sky above and the region below the earth—they called *Duant*. During the daylight hours, Ra sailed over the sky from East to West in the Boat of Day, setting at last in the Western horizon. Ra then entered the Boat of Night and began his journey through the *Duant* across the waters of the nether sky below the earth.[3]

During the New Kingdom period (18th Dynasty, ca. 1400 B.C.E.), the *Duant* became the focus of a new type of sacred text that explored the nocturnal journey of the Sun through the Netherworld. The two primary examples are *The Book of the Pylons* (also known as *The Book of Gates*) and *The Book of what is in the Duant* (sometimes called *Amduat*). The nighttime passage of the Sun described in these books was intended to signify the path of the human soul after death; the soul could experience a rebirth from the depths of darkness and be reborn like the Sun itself. This is clearly indicated to us by the fact that in these texts the Sun is depicted with the head of a Ram. The word for "ram" is 𓃝 "Ba," and "Ba," spelled 𓅽 or 𓅡, is also the word for "soul."[4]

---

[3] James Allen, *Middle Egyptian,* p. 21.
[4] Psychologically, the *Ba,* as a human-headed bird 𓅽 (often accompanied by a bowl of incense), represented the soul's flight from Consciousness into the Unconscious. *Ba,* represented as the saddle-billed stork 𓅡, signified the soul as a living but unconscious element; the *Ba*

In terms of modern analytical psychology, the *Duant* is one representation of the Unconscious, the "underworld," inhabited by gods and dæmons, living symbols that we call primordial images or Archetypes.[5] This journey of the Sun described in the books of the netherworld thus not only represents the passage of the human soul after death, but also that of a descent into the Unconscious.

It is probable that the origin of *The Book of Pylons* occurred during the Amarna period of the revolutionary Pharaoh Akhenaten (ca. 1353–1336 B.C.E.). An incomplete example of this text is found in the sarcophagus chamber in the tomb of Pharaoh Haremhab (ca. 1323–1295 B.C.E.) who succeeded Tutankhamun (ca. 1336–1327 B.C.E.). It also occurs later in the tombs of Rameses I (ca. 1295–1294 B.C.E.) through Rameses VI (ca. 1143–1136 B.C.E.).

At a very early point in the scholastic evaluation of *The Book of Pylons*, scholars were struck by the appearance of the "four races" of the world shown in the Fifth Pylon. The Egyptians themselves (not just the King), as well as Asiatics, Nubians and Libyans, were welcomed to enter the Pylons, for all were said to have come into being from Horus who protects their *Ba*-souls. Such a catholic and benevolent representation stands in stark contrast to the exclusionary concepts by which the ancient Egyptians had always set themselves above and apart from the rest of the world. The word the Egyptians used for themselves, *remethu*, literally meant "human beings." Everyone not an Egyptian traditionally had been considered sub-human.

Yet, in *The Book of Pylons* we find the remarkable depiction

---

as a Ram accompanied by a bowl of incense, signified the human soul as Libido.

[5] For a scholarly and thoughtful translation of *The Book of Amduat* that gives due consideration to the viewpoint of Jungian analytical psychology see Andreas Schweizer, *The Sun God's Journey through the Netherworld: Reading the Ancient Egyptian Amduat*.

The Four Races of Man depicted in the Fifth Pylon.
(Based on the mural in the tomb of Sety I.)

of other peoples of the world, all welcomed to follow the path of the human Soul with the declaration that they are all children of the same God. It is this amazingly cosmopolitan view that makes it likely this book came into existence due to the influence of the heretic Pharoah Akhenaten.[6] In fact, it was this very inclusive attitude that originally led me to believe that entrance to the Pylons was still possible and open for investigation. And so it was that I began my exploration of the Starry Abode in 1975 E.V.

---

[6] Cf. *The Great Hymn to the Aten* composed by the Pharoah Akhenaten in Miriam Lichtheim, *Ancient Egyptian Literature, Vol. II. The New Kingdom*, pp. 96–100. Lichtheim described this hymn as expressing "the cosmopolitan and humanist outlook of the New Kingdom at its purest and most sympathetic. All peoples are seen as the creatures of the sun god, who has made them diverse in skin color, speech, and character. Their diversity is described objectively, without a claim of Egyptian superiority."

The first examined hieroglyphic text of *The Book of Pylons* was that from the tomb of Rameses VI, translated by Jean-François Champollion in his thirteenth letter from Egypt in 1829.[7] The first known complete version of *The Book of Pylons* was found engraved on the sarcophagus of Pharaoh Sety I (ca. 1290–1279 B.C.E.). In 1864, Joseph Bonomi and Samuel Sharpe published the text and illustrations of *The Book of Gates* from this sarcophagus without translation.[8] Their publication is still considered the authoritative edition of the Egyptian original.

The work by Bonomi and Sharp was used by Eugène Lefébure for his translation published under the title *The Book of Hades* in 1878 and 1881,[9] and Gaston Maspero's study published in *Revue de l'histoire des religions* in 1888.[10] In 1905, E.A. Wallis Budge published a translation of the sarcophagus of Sety I.[11] The two latter translations are not only outdated, they are unreliable. For example, for Pylons number two through six, Lefébure and Budge both gave the incorrect names for the Pylons as well as their Guardians. They mistakenly assigned the name of Pylon Two and its Guardian to Pylon Three, the correct name of Pylon Three and its Guardians to Pylon Four, and so on, until Pylon Six where the correct order was ascertained. The lid of the sarcophagus of Sety I, when found, was broken into several pieces. This fragmented condition resulted in the translators reading an incorrect sequence.

---

[7] Champollion, *Lettres ecrites d'Égypte et de Nubie en 1828 et 1829*, pp. 182 ff.
[8] Joseph Bonomi and Samuel Sharpe, *The Alabaster Sarcophagus of Oimeneptah I, King of Egypt*.
[9] Eugène Lefébure, *The Book of Hades* in *Records of the Past*, Vols. 10 and 12.
[10] *Les Hypogées Royaux de Thèbes* in *Revue de l'histoire des religions*, Vol 17, pp. 251–310. Cf. Also Jéquier, *Le Livre de ce qu'il y a dans l'Hades*.
[11] Budge, *The Egyptian Heaven and Hell*, Vols. 2 and 3.

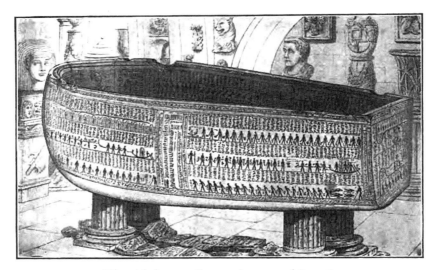

The Alabaster Sarcophagus of Sety I.

The first synoptic edition of *The Book of Pylons*, compiled from all known sources, was published by Charles Maystre and Alexandre Piankoff in *Mémoires publiés par les membres de l'Institut français d'archéologie orientale du Caire* [MIFAO], nos. 74, 75 and 90 (1939–1962) and *Annales du service des antiquités de l'Égypte* No. 55 [ASAE] (1958).

At the time of these magical workings, the book by Bonomi and Sharpe and the works by Maystre and Piankoff were the only reliable resources available. They have since been replaced by Erik Hornung's *The Egyptian Book of Gates* (2014). Hornung had previously noted that *The Book of the Pylons* (and the other books of its type such as the *Amduat*, *The Book of Caverns*, and *The Book of the Earth*), were the first religious books of the ancient Egyptians whose content was permanent and unchanging.[12] This is different from the collection of spells of *The Book*

---

[12] There is nevertheless a long illustrated version of *Amduat*, as well as a short version containing no pictures. For a complete list of available publications, see Erik Hornung, *The Ancient Egyptian Books of the*

of the Dead, for example, which underwent constant modification. Furthermore, the illustrations of these Pylon texts were also more than mere vignettes. They and the text formed a unified whole.[13] These documents are generally known as *The Books of the Netherworld*.

* * *

Throughout these Visions, especially in the beginning, I encountered a number of instructional speeches that represent expressions of the *paradoxia*—a motif that exhibits seemingly self-contradictory but equally valued elements. These were working examples of the Unconscious seeking to establish a condition of wholeness. The large majority of these are quite elementary in form. This is particularly fitting since I was quite young. Despite their simplicity, they nevertheless represent spontaneous expressions of the Unconscious trying to redress the balance of the psyche, and in that sense, they are interesting examples. At the time, I considered many of these speeches puerile and repetitious; I found the language to be pretentious and florid. However, for some unknown reason, this seems to be characteristic of the language of the Unconscious; lofty and often pompous, or stylistically structured after the manner of the King James Bible.[14]

Confronting the Unconscious can be exhilarating and fulfilling, but at the same time it can be perilous, and due caution must be taken. For this reason, students of Magick are prepared by training in Rituals of Banishing, which can serve as bastions against the dangers of the unconscious void. Jung emphasized that the Unconscious itself is neutral; its normal function is to compensate the conscious condition. On the other hand, the Unconscious is dangerous when the conscious state is in conflict with the true nature. This is true of all of us to some degree when

---

[13] Erik Hornung, *The Ancient Egyptian Books of the Afterlife*, p. 26.
[14] See Carl Jung, *Memories, Dreams, Reflections*, pp. 177–178. Jung had the same experience with the language of Archetypes.

we are seeking to discover our Pure Will—which is in fact our "true nature." But if the conscious position is considerably out of balance, the reaction of the Unconscious may be extremely disquieting. For such individuals, invasion by unconscious content may cause abject fear and panic, or in extreme cases, a potential psychosis.[15] This is one of the main reasons the schools of Initiation stress the importance of having a solid and well-adjusted life in the mundane world before attempting to practice Magick.

At the time of this experiment I functioned primarily on what we call the Magical or Egyptian plane.[16] This is not to say that all of the symbolism contained herein is strictly Egyptian. Indeed, there is much that is veiled in symbolism totally foreign to the Egyptian school. However, the underlying element woven throughout the Magical language of this document, which serves as its foundation, finds its origin in Egyptian Theurgy.

Certain other aspects, even though spiritually diverse, are Archetypes that became dynamized by Egyptian factors once they entwined with consciousness within my psyche. The manifestations of Archetypes are not static or perpetually homologous. Rather, they are like living aggregates that continually expand and evolve within the psychosoma of the individual. Time has shown that many of the images represented herein are harmonious with my personal psyche—not surprisingly since I am the one who obtained these visions. There are also many components of these visions that represented the limitations of my current incarnation. At the time of these Workings, I had not yet attained to the Knowledge and Conversation of the Holy Guardian Angel. Thus, there is a distinct immaturity represented at various points in this Record, in the early Visions in particular.

Anyone attempting a similar experiment should not expect his or her visions to be identical to mine in either content or

---

[15] Jung, *Mysterium Coniunctionis*, pp. 156 ff. See also Jung, *Man and his Symbols*, p. 37, paragraph 2.
[16] See *Book IV*, Part III, Appendix III.

character. Certain analogies will likely occur, especially in what concerns some of the more general mysteries encountered. But in some cases, they may not correspond at all.

The only justification for publishing a work of this type lies in the fact that it is, for better or worse, the accurate result of an experiment. If we hope to gain knowledge of the unknown regions of the psyche, we must not shrink from making public our findings—complete with accounts of our failures as well as our successes. Examples of both instances are fully documented here. My dialogue in the Visions has been edited at times to give clarity. However, the Angelic speeches have been retained exactly as they occurred.[17]

While conducting this experiment, I originally believed that the first four Pylons of the *Duant* represented Gateways to the final four Sephiroth on the Tree of Life. At this stage in the experiment, I submitted this Record to my Instructor in the A∴A∴ for review. Frater Adjuvo (Marcelo Ramos Motta) disagreed and advised me that in his considered opinion, the first four Pylons were the Four Gates of Malkuth and referred to the four Elements thereof. He encouraged me to continue this experiment. After taking up the Work again, I explored the next three Pylons, which I discovered corresponded to Yesod, Hod and Netzach. The first four Pylons do indeed correspond to the Four Gates of Malkuth, but they also receive reflections of higher Sephiroth and Paths. But more than this, the Pylons contain internal gateways or Pylons that lead to higher planes on the Tree of Life without consideration of the Paths. These "higher planes" include the Thirty Æthyrs. For example, the Fourth Pylon, while corresponding to the Fire quadrant of Malkuth, can give entrance into the Sephira Netzach, and possibly Geburah.

Further experimentation must be done along this line of inquiry. However, it is clear from practice that the Pylons have

---

[17] Angelic renderings of Egyptian god names proved challenging. They were recorded as closely as possible to how they sounded.

a distinct analogy to the scientific theory of "wormholes," a hypothetical gateway through spacetime. The influence of the Paths is ever-present, but often in unexpected ways, and always as a "reflection," rather than a route of passage. Likewise, the intersection of the Æthyrs and Tree of Life may be perceived in the Pylons, but is thus far impossible to describe in language or in diagram. In one of the Visions, I was shown a map of this intersection, but was unable to render it in two dimensions. (The map, shown by the Angel, was probably in four dimensions and thus impossible to render in three dimensions—certainly not in two.)

In this particular Record, only the first seven Pylons are explored. At that time, I was not admitted to those Pylons beyond, save for a fleeting glimpse of the Holy Bridal Chamber (Tiphereth).

It will be noted that varying periods of time separate these attempts at exploration, sometimes lasting several months. This was not because I lost interest in the experiment. It will be seen that after exploring the first four Pylons, a period of six months elapsed before the practice was resumed. I discovered that before further workings could be undertaken, the previous Visions required consolidation. Without this vital aspect of integration, proceeding into the more complex areas of the Pylons was impossible. I was literally barred from entrance. This was especially true after the first four Pylons. My vehicle, coming into contact with a higher "resonance," as it were, suffered a shock which required harmonization. This was due to my inability to withstand *samādhi*. The energy, instead of being silently and totally absorbed, was channeled into the *nāḍīs*, a common problem for beginners.

The ability to withstand the various trances can take years to accomplish in some cases. When I had managed to integrate the experiences, or at least a substantial portion of them, I found that entrance to the succeeding levels was effortless. I was literally flung into the Pylons by my natural momentum.

It has been my experience that, generally speaking, a true vision does not require strenuous effort to obtain, unless the difficulty is integral to the vision itself. The vision will occur spontaneously if the Banishings and Invocations have been properly performed. Attempts to force visions can result in Astral "creation" rather than experiencing a genuine vision. This should be avoided at all costs, for it is altogether too easy to mold a vision that follows pathways of prejudice or misconceptions of one's own Universe.

Furthermore, the student must be in control at all times; for he or she will be tested at every turn. The ability to GO where one wills to go is essential and is the keynote to a successful Astral exploration. This requirement should be satisfied by a thorough practice of the instructions in "Liber O." That being said, it should be noted that the Visions of the Pylons are not strictly Astral; as I noted above, there are areas within the Pylons that extend beyond what we call the Astral Plane to the deeper regions of the Sephiroth as well as the Æthyrs. These regions are more difficult to navigate, and the Guardians are diligent in their task to keep out the unworthy or the foolhardy.

* * *

A word must be said about the interpretation of Visions, for this too is an aspect of integrating the experience. Without this ability—which must be cultivated by practice and introspection—the seeds of insight are cast on barren ground. I was once told by my Instructor, "Anybody can have visions, but only the wise, or the foolish, can interpret them."

Upon returning to read these Visions for the first time after twenty-five years, I was surprised to discover the rudiments of insights which over the years had become an integral part of my Initiatic life. At the time of the Visions, many of these things were completely beyond my ability to comprehend. One might say it merely took twenty-five years to consolidate the Instruction before I had the wit to understand what had been given to me so long before. Because I understood so little, I considered these Visions worthless and put them away for almost three decades. I remarked to one of my Students that this Record was not worth the paper on which it was written. The Student politely disagreed and urged me to reconsider it. This reconsideration has, at last, resulted in this publication. It will rest with others to determine the value, if any, these Visions have for them. More importantly, it is hoped they will lead to further experimentation and understanding of these mysterious realms. Pylons Eight through Twelve remain to be explored and documented.

This document is in A∴A∴ Class C. That being said, it is worthwhile to note that the Angelic cries of the Second Part of the Sixth Pylon should be considered authentic and true up to the Grade of Exempt Adept.

Concerning the *modus operandi* whereby the Talismans may be formed and the Visions obtained, the complete instructions are given in Appendices 1–6.

Serving as my Scribe was my dear friend, assistant and Student, the late Richard Gernon, Frater I.A.T.A. ("I await the awaking"). Richard was the ideal Scribe: well-versed in Qabalah, Tarot and the general methods and history of the Western Magical tradition, he also was familiar with Middle Egyptian, Coptic and Greek. I believe "Gurney" would applaud making this Record public after so many years. His assistance in this experiment was incalculable, his counsel always sound, and his enthusiasm for the completion of this Work was unwavering.

* * *

To Hymenaeus Beta, Frater Superior Ordo Templi Orientis, I offer my sincere thanks for permission to reproduce the images of the Thoth Tarot Deck. Frater V.V. generously provided needed materials and much appreciated editorial skills. The late Frater Y. kindly read early proofs and offered many helpful suggestions.

Frater I.A.T.A., Richard William Gernon, the Scribe.

I would like to thank Yvonne Paglia for her unwavering support which has given me the opportunity to reach the world. I owe so much to the late Donald Weiser whose Work placed the Wisdom of the Sages within my reach, and whose friendship will be sorely missed. Special thanks to Momo Avram, Gwen Gunther, Ian Mercer, Jasenka Milosovic, and Nancy Wasserman for the original artwork. Momo Avram and the late Angel Lorenz generously provided assistance with Enochian research. Stephen King encouraged me to make this work public and his excitement about continuing the exploration of the Pylons is deeply appreciated. J.P. Lund, Ian Mercer, Marko Milenovic, Santo Rizzuto, Giuseppe Zappia and Tikki Zappia read the proofs and contributed many corrections. Thanks as ever to James

Wasserman for his editing skill, and for his patience with the difficulties of the complex typography that are known to accompany my work. My very special thanks to Giuseppe Zappia for the wonderful surprise of secretly commissioning the portrait *The Magician* by Robert Buratti, and to Robert himself for the gift which demonstrates his magnificent talent. I was deeply touched by such a generous, thoughtful act and I will forever treasure this work of art. Lastly, I am grateful to my wife Gwen for her artwork, invaluable advice, encouragement, and her endless fount of inspiration.

For any who hold these pages, I now leave them in your hands. Make of them what you will.

Love is the law, love under will.

—J. Daniel Gunther
April 8, 2018 e.v.

The Visions of the Pylons

A Magical Record of Exploration in the Starry Abode

August 22, 1975 E.V.
to February 5, 1977 E.V.

J. Daniel Gunther

A∴A∴ Publication in Class C

V.	7°=4□	Praemonstrator
V.V.	6°=5□	Imperator
Y.	5°=6□	Cancellarius

So came I to Duant, the starry abode,
and I heard voices crying aloud.

—Liber LXV, II:2

I AM TAKEN TO TRAVERSE what seems to be a great distance and enter into the domain of the First Pylon. And the Voice of the Angel of the Pylon says:

> "This word 'Pylon' is a mockery in this place, for she who is the daughter has no part of the Golden Rod for she is barren as yet.[1] She is the virgin daughter of Hades who is not mentioned by name. For in her countenance is found all manner of beauties and all manner of distortions."[2]

I see myself girt about with chains and chains and chains. Although I struggle to free myself I cannot. There is darkness and loneliness and the breath of Dragons in this place. And I understand only in part, seeing the remainder as if not at all.[3]

And the Angel says:

> "This is well, for thou dost see what is and what is girt about with tribulations and what is poured into the Lesser Cup. There is poison and pollution for the fools, yet there

---

[1] The word "Pylon" is derived from the Greek πύλη, which means "gate" or "doorway." It may also have the meaning of "orifice." This Pylon is referred to ה final of יהוה, i.e. Malkuth, and in particular to the Earth quadrant thereof. The "Golden Rod" refers to the cult phallus of Osiris whereby Horus was conceived. Cf. *Liber VII*, VII:5.

[2] Here is the first example of the *Paradoxia*.

[3] The threefold mention of "chains" indicates Daäth. This chain symbolically has 333 links. In the sense here, it refers to the inert and immobile qualities found in earth. It is the nature of incarnation, and might well be called the "chains of *saṃsāra*" (संसार, "wandering"). The "breath of Dragons" refers to Leviathan = לויתן = 496 = מלכות "Malkuth."

is ambrosia and wine for the wise. She who is the Crone to the many is a Bride to the few."[4]

I see her of whom he speaks and she is crowned with a garland of flowers and upon her gown are two scarlet arrows that point unto her feet. At the hem of her garment there are serpents with dragon heads and open mouths like Leviathan who is in the sea.[5]

The Angel spoke again and said:

"She is the sea. Those who perceive it not have crusted over the crystal waters with the spittle from their vulgar mouths and with their feces and with their blasphemies. She will be redeemed from their curses by the Beast of the Four who will devour their desecrations in the lust of his anger, and they shall be no more."[6]

I am allowed to see this creature of whom he speaks, but he seems tame and without malice.

---

[4] The "lesser cup" = ה final of יהוה. The implication is "The daughter (Malkuth) is the Mother (Binah)." Cf. the Mystic Readings of the Alphabet for ה spelled in full. Here are more examples of the *Paradoxia*. The gross qualities of the "lower self" (poison and pollution) must be transmuted to the highest (ambrosia and wine). To those who do not dare (the "fools," the "many") the daughter is a "Crone." She is a "Bride" to the few, that is, Neophytes. The reference comes from Hecate, the tripartite goddess of witchcraft who is maid, mother and crone.

[5] Malkah (מלכה) the Queen, a name for Malkuth as Bride of Microprosopus. She wears a robe suggestive of Binah and the Robe of the Magister Templi, but with dual Arrows and multiple serpents at the hem of her garment. This indicates that aspiration was not yet unified for myself. Leviathan again confirms Malkuth.

[6] The profane are incapable of seeing holiness in the lowest form of manifestation. The Beast of the Four is the Sphinx, which represents the harmonious balance of the elements.

And the Angel said:

"It is well, for thou art written in the Book of Salvations and doth not tempt the Beast with provocations or veils or wine that is but the urine of the Cocatrice. For he is *all* of these and *none* of these and those who believe this not are bound by the infirmity that he carries like a plague."[7]

Now I have seen this plague, like a horde of swarming things — locusts and grasshoppers and vile insects with claws that rend and tear and from whose mouth run foul excretions. I have seen them upon the bloated bellies of the carrion stinking in the fields and lying dead with their treasures.[8]

"Lo!," saith the Angel, "There cometh an Oracle!"

I see a most beautiful woman who wears a white gown and who carries herself like a queen. Her head is entirely bare, her hands are empty and her feet are not shod.[9]

There is writing upon the front of her gown and it reads:

---

[7] Another *Paradoxia*. I was being shown an elementary vision dealing with the flexibility of the Universe. The phrase "Book of Salvations" is oddly out of place, and was clearly an intellectual intrusion due to my Christian childhood, although the phrase is not typical in the doctrine of my youth. Another word was actually used by the Angel, possibly "Salutations."

[8] These words arose spontaneously while the accompanying vision was that of a normal countryside. Most likely, my Ruach was attempting to disrupt the actual message of the Vision, hence the Oracle that follows immediately.

[9] Another vision of Malkah, this time from the viewpoint of Malkuth. Bare head, empty hands and bare feet indicate her essential purity. There is also a further meaning, which she later provides by a hint.

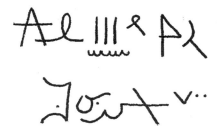

And this is the transliteration thereof:

ACHHAShNV
shiivl
SHEETrIFEE

Now I thought to Record the meaning of this, as it had been made known to me, but I found that I could not."[10]

She begins to speak:

"Those who stumble at this Pylon stumble because they strive to write their names in blood upon it. But it turneth into a stinking black slime that devours them with all manner of foul deaths. Here they must bind themselves with Oaths and Promises and discard the faith of the slaves. For he who treads upon this ground must cast off his shoes and turn not back for any. Here, darkness is desirable and to be lust after. Here, Set deflowers the daughter of the God and fills her with his seed. Here is

---

[10] The translation of this script was revealed at the time of the Vision, but when I attempted to transmit it to normal consciousness, I found no bridge whereby to pass the information. The meaning would return twelve years later. It was a personal prophecy that meant, "the Child of Nu, the water-crosser, is summoned." The meaning returned only after the prophecy was fulfilled. I was told that an Oracle was coming and this indicated the script in question.

but the reflection of Knowledge in the waters of the Lesser Sea."[11]

I see her wrap her arms about herself and see them become great white wings. Her countenance alters until she becomes a dragon-faced demon that frightens me and makes me seek safety. She has sexual organs like a man—a great red phallus of stone upon which I see carved a word: ΘΕΛΗΜΑ.

I do not comprehend the meaning of this. She laughs an awful laugh, a mocking laugh, squeezes her breasts, and pus runs out instead of milk. She has cloven hooves like a goat or satyr. She begins to rave and shriek until I am lost in this madness![12]

The Angel reappears[13] and says:

"Speak the Word."

I say the Word, though I fear the result: "*Thelema.*"

Then all becomes quiet. the Dragon-Beast-Queen is no more. She has returned unto her former self and she smiles a strange smile at me. I feel like a great fool and am ashamed that I did not know the answer to this great riddle.[14]

---

[11] The writing in blood refers to the legend of the first Passover, in which the lintels of the door (pylon) were stained with blood to ward off the Angel of Death. Cf. *Liber 418*, 12th Æthyr. Whosoever takes the Oath of the Neophyte must one day enter the Chapel of Abominations. Yet, I was told that here is only the reflection of Daäth in ה final, the "lesser sea."

[12] Once again, the *Paradoxia*.

[13] Note that no account is given of the Angel's departure.

[14] Clearly, at some level, I was afraid of Thelema, even afraid to merely utter the word. This fear is not uncommon when aspirants first come into contact with Thelema. It is unconscious fear of ego destruction. Cf. *Liber Tzaddi* 16–20. Later, during certain Initiations, this fear takes on new dimensions. Cf. *Liber LXV*, IV:30–40 and V:31–36. In any case, it is sheer courage and nothing else that one can rely on. The Initiator has

But the Angel spoke and said:

"Ye knew it and spake it."

Yet, I pressed close to the Angel and inquired of him, "Will I not be able to pass this Pylon lest I give its name?"

The Angel answered me:

"It is so, but thou hast written that name as an Image like unto thyself."

I see the Pylon that is a great white obelisk upon which is patterned the image of the Aten with Rays terminating in hands.
 I speak unto the Angel: "This is an ancient stone, yet it is not weather-beaten or scarred or defiled."
 The Angel answered:

"It is so, for as it was said in the presence of Neferu-Ha-Neter, the priestess of the Shrine of Hut-Hooru, thou would come to pass to be Heru[15] in the Age of Light. Thus, the writing faded not. For that which was carved in the City of the Sun is carved in the core of thine heart and cannot be lost or abandoned. Thus it was that the Word Thelema was uttered, for this is what hath brought thee thus far.

---

no pity, for our condition is a byproduct of our own Oath and Task, and we are obligated to fulfill it.

[15] The spellings of these Egyptian words are only an approximation of the actual pronunciation heard. The name Neferu-Ha-Neter was apparently the personal name of a priestess of 𓉡, Hathor, given here as Hut-Hooru. The name Heru indicates a form of Horus, and the "Age of Light" signifies the Æon of the Child. This refers to one of my previous incarnations.

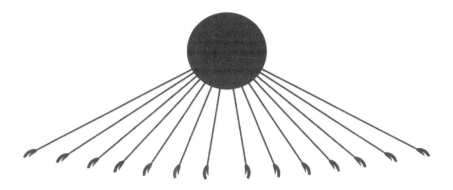

Leave this place now. Return unto thine abode and remain for a space until the Gateway of the Second Pylon is opened during the time of the Moon."

And I return, though sadly, for I feel a great longing. But I know that this is the longing of the memory and not of the Will. Thus, it is lost in the path that I have taken.

August 22, 1975 e.v.
12:00 p.m. – 1:00 p.m.

Now I am taken to tread the path leading to the Second Pylon. The Pylon looms ahead, built of great stone like the sanctuary of the Druids.¹

By shape, it is the letter Cheth ח, and upon it in the center is graven the symbol of the lunar crescent beneath an emblem of the sun.²

To the left of this symbol there is engraved the word³

$$\mathrm{NAKHEShT}$$

I pressed unto the Angel of the Pylon and said, "Bring unto me the guardian of this place so that its mystery should be divulged."

And the Angel said,

"It is so."

Suddenly, I am aware of an incredible motion, as if the entire Aire was spinning at a great rate of speed. The Pylon before me begins to crumble and fall, breaking into great pieces of stone and debris.⁴

---

[1] The pylon had the shape of a portion of Stonehenge.

[2] The shape of the Pylon suggests Cheth, referred to ♋ Cancer, the house of the Moon. This Pylon being △ of ▽ receives a reflection from Yesod and ☽.

[3] NAKHEShT = נאכהשט = 385. Note that 385 is also the numeration of שכינה "Shekinah," a synonym for Adonai, the Holy Guardian Angel, and ΙΕΡΟΣ, "holy." NAKHEShT may be interpreted NOX-ה-☿. The emblem ☿ is a form of the Sun in the arms of the Moon, or Kteis under Phallos. Cf. *Liber VII*, VI:1–7.

[4] The motion is due to the reflection of Luna, which traverses the Zodiac faster than any planet. Likewise, the element Air is related to

The earth is riven open and I see corpses rise up from the hollow earth. They wear white gowns or robes and they stare into the heavens. Then, silver stars and stones begin to rain upon them, showering them with its burden, but they remain motionless.[5]

The entire Aire is still spinning. Above, in the sky, I now see an enormous sun, luminous and blazing with a great light. Then it explodes, but without sound! And now it appears to be an illusion and that it is really a moon, cratered and barren and void of life. The Aire ceases its motion.[6]

The risen corpses are now passed away. They are but grinning skulls within empty robes.[7] In their hands they each hold an object which I cannot see well enough to perceive its purpose.

The Angel said:

"Move closer."

---

the opposites of Flux and Reflux. There is also a reflection of פ which is symbolically the "roof" of Yesod. יסוד "Yesod" and פ "Peh" both = 80. Compare the crumbling of the Pylon with Atu XVI, the destruction of the House of God.

[5] The risen corpses are suggestive of the old form of Atu XX, "Judgment." Here, the corpses represent the ministers of the Æon of Osiris; they stare into the heavens seeking redemption from without rather than within. They do not know that the Khabs is in the Khu. The kisses of the stars rain hard upon them but they do not comprehend it. They stare into the heavens searching for a redeemer that will not come. Also, they remain "motionless"; that is, they do not GO.

[6] The sun exploding without sound is symbolic of the Lingam, the Word whose Speech is Silence. At the time of the Vision, I suddenly thought of *Liber A'ash*, verse 16: "Understand that the yielding of the Yoni is one with the lengthening of the Lingam."

[7] The passing of the Æon of Osiris. The external hull of their doctrine remains in the world but there is no life within. The ☠ *Caput Mortuum*, "Dead Head" (or plural, as in the Vision, *Capita Mortua*) anciently signified the head of Osiris. It also appears in Alchemy as the symbol ⊙ which signifies "worthless residue."

Trump XX — Le Jugement
Jean Dodal Tarot (early 18th century E.V.)

I do so. Now, they appear to be large pearls, larger than I have ever seen.

The Angel speaks and says:

"They are eggs and not stone; not jewels but shell; not valued by the merchant or seaman, but by the carrion birds of the field. There are their offspring in this cradle, awaiting the coming warmth to renew their life. But it shall come not, for here is Sterility. Thus, these eggs are the eggs of the desert. If they hatch, they hatch out Dragons who live but to die and who vomit water and pass blood."[8]

Now I hear a throng of shrieking birds and the sky is turned black by their wings.
  The Angel says:

"It is the return of the Harpies and the beast birds of Hecate their mother. They have come to devour the dead that hold the eggs."[9]

I turn and flee down a long, endless road, fearing that these birds will find me as prey. At last, I come to a crossroads where three roads meet.[10] There is a large entity standing by the roadside. He begins to speak:

---

[8] The pearl is the stone of the Moon. However, the Angel states clearly that they were eggs and not stone, not jewels but shell. It was illusion. This is in keeping with the nature of Luna which can be a world of *deceptio visûs* and phantasmagoria. Things are not always what they seem. Ministers of the Æon of Osiris think they hold the egg of Spirit but are deceived. They are but the eggs of the Shells, the Qliphoth. The Angel says they are not valued by the merchant (Cf. *Liber LXV*, V:20) or the seaman (Masters of the Temple upon the Great Sea of Binah). The desert is a symbol of the Abyss which is reflected after a certain manner in Yesod, and thus in Air of Earth. The "eggs" of the Qliphoth hatch out only the offspring of fatality. Water and blood signify the essences of life which they are not able to retain.

[9] The carrion birds whose eggs are held by the dead are the Qliphoth, several aspects of which are depicted as black, noisy birds. Cf. *Liber DCCCXIII*, II:4–7, and the legend of Phineas and the Harpies in Greek mythology.

[10] A place of three crossroads is traditionally sacred to Hecate. Once again, I demonstrated fear by running. The Angel stated that the

Harpies in the infernal wood
by Gustave Doré from Canto XIII of Dante's *Inferno*.

"Begone, my child. For thou dost seek my mother, the goddess of the stars and not her sister of the thorny brow."

I know of whom he speaks, so I answer him, the words being

---

birds would devour the dead holding the eggs, i.e. the Qliphoth. The action was an unconscious one, but revealing. I instinctively knew that I was wallowing in the world of the Qliphoth, and feared my own destruction.

placed within my mind from some point beyond.[11] "I have conquered this bitch of damnation who driveth men mad who do not speak to her with averted face. I have feasted upon her worm-eaten flesh to appease her savage lust. I have won at the games that make babbling fools of the lofty. I am not beguiled by her toothless grin. This path have I trod centuries before now. I have but returned this way for a space, for my journey lies beyond the Veil as thou sayest, beyond the Mountain, beyond the Rose and beyond the Sorrow thronged about her Throne who is the Queen of the NOX. I await Sekhmet and her sister Bast, for them will I love and devour with my lust. They are not barren and shall yield me a child. Then shall the Foundation be firm."[12]

The Watcher speaks:[13]

> "This is more than Foundation, what is the center spoke of the Rose."

And I challenged him saying, "Thou liest! For Hadit is the center therein as it is written in our holiest book! This is but the

---

[11] I assumed the reference was to Hecate, not realizing that I was being tested. Hecate and Nuit are not sisters; they are one. The "point" was not "beyond" at all, as practice of *Liber XVI* later proved.

[12] I was still afraid, and this inflated speech is an attempt to bluff the Angel. It is an example of the Ego attempting to regain control of the situation. The speech is so childish it is not worth comment.

[13] Note that I initially referred to this being as simply an "entity." Now, for no apparent reason, I used the term "Watcher." If this title was transmitted to me at some point, I retained no memory of it. According to legend, the ἐγρήγοροι or "watchers" were a group of so-called "fallen angels" who mated with human women and gave birth to the נפילים Nephilim (Cf. Genesis 6:1–4). See the first and second Book of Enoch and Jubilees for this term. However, in the book of Daniel, the term occurs in the Aramaic word עיר, which is used to indicate an "Angel." This is the sense implied in this Vision.

The Tripartite Hecate — Maiden, Mother, and Crone.

outer edge of the Abyss, the lady who is the giver of form and the taker of stability."[14]

Again, he speaks to me and says:

---

[14] At the time, I had mistakenly attributed this Pylon to Yesod proper. I also did not understand the nature of Hadit at that time. Thus, the Watcher follows with an Instruction.

"Come closer to me."

He takes out from his robe a large shew-stone, and he says:

"I will grant unto thee the innermost vision of the sphere and the edges of the Aire that it doth touch in the name of our Lord *Shaddai El-Chai.*"[15]

As I peer into the stone he utters the word:

"QUEShEMANAMAH"[16]

The stone stirs. This is the Vision thereof:
I see a grinning dæmon of immense size with his fingers locked together somewhat like a *mudra*. Yet, he is playing a child's game and seeks to show me his strategies. And he sings:

"Here is the church and here is the steeple!
Open the doors and here are the people!"

He begins to laugh.
I continue to stare into the stone even though I have heard this riddle before, having played this game as a child and finding no truth therein.
The dæmon of the stone no longer smiles, and he stares into his empty hands, crushing them together. He speaks:

---

[15] שדי אל חי, the God Name of Yesod in Assiah. (Cf. *Liber 777*, Col. 5.)
[16] QUEShEMANAMAH = קואשהמאנאמה = 550 = 55 × 10 (the Mystic number of Malkuth multiplied by the number of Malkuth). The numeration was not discovered until after the first four Pylons were explored. I should have examined this word Qabalistically immediately after the Vision. This might have been a hint to me since it is not a number proper to Yesod. Yet, it is also a clue to a reflection from Geburah which is revealed a bit later.

"Thus it is written that the children are prophets to the wise. Who hath the wit to hear the marvel from the mouths of babes? Fool! They who have laughed at my honor shall be buried in the ant-heap and devoured by the insects of the earth! That which was stable shall fall! My Voice which is Silence doth move and shatter the established mountains. Thus at the entrance of the Aire didst thou see the Pylon fall. Take this stone and rebuild it in my name and in my glory."[17]

I beseeched him saying, "What is thy name? Give this unto me so that I may write it upon the gateway of the stars and upon the cornerstone of the temple."

The dæmon says:

"Thou knowest! For my mother is EIGHTY and I am her blazing Child of the Tower.[18] Herein am I imprisoned in this stone mansion, not against my Will, but with full Motion of my Will. For this Tower is but the image of my Will[19] and therein will I remain until the Word is uttered

---

[17] The Angel identifies with the Word of the New Æon which brought the destruction of the Old Æon. Cf. *Liber VII*, IV:44.

[18] The "mother" = Yesod = יסוד = 80, which is also the value of פ, Atu XVI, "The Tower."

[19] I.e., the ΦΑΛΛΟΣ.

and I am shot forth, an arrow from the Sun into the mouth of the dead father.[20] Thus dost thou learn of the edges of the Æthyrs and Aires and how they infringe one upon the other. For my name is WARLORD and DRAGON, LORD OF THE RED PLANET and CHILD OF THE MOON,[21] the MASTER OF THE EARTH from whence thou didst come first. For my name is likewise 19 which is also the name of my mother whom I have manifest from my image.[22] I am indeed the Lord of the stone into which thou gazest, and I am the prophet of thy task. There are ways in which my mother and I are alike. We are both MOTION, she to the Aire, and I to the point, I who am also JUSTICE.[23] For she is the moon, cold and barren, but I am the blood therein. The best blood cometh therefrom monthly when her motion ceaseth. Then do I leap out and devour the worshippers! Then is the sorcery deified and thus is she redeemed from her witchcrafts. Then is her number squared and I leap forth erect and glad![24] Therefore also is a mystery of the lunar cave of my father CHAOS and the child that cometh not. Child of Sorrow and Sorrow and Sorrow and breeder of monsters! For 81 is he also, but devoid of my mother's womb.[25] Thus dost thou learn to see the facets of the stone: the flat which is round and

---

[20] See the Sixth Pylon, Part 2, page 120.

[21] All references to a reflection from Geburah and Peh = ♂.

[22] The name equating to 19 suggested by the Angel is still unclear, but the name of the mother indicated is Eve, חוה = 19. The word Eve means "to manifest."

[23] The mother as a reflection of Yesod = Air = motion. The Son as a reflection of Geburah = matter in motion. "Justice" = דין, a name of Geburah.

[24] The number 9^2 = 81. The 80 of פ "The Tower" with 1 erect and glad.

[25] The reference is to the 3 of Swords, "Sorrow," and the formula of אלים. Cf. *Book IV*, Part III, Chapter IV.

Atu XVI: The Tower — Thoth Tarot

The 3 of Swords — Thoth Tarot

the square which is divided, the waters which are blood and the tears which are moons, the dead which are also risen in my name. For I am that blazing one hidden in the mask of sterility.[26]

Go! Quit this place, for the ceremony is ended! The Temple is rebuilded and the earth is closed again. The writing on the stone is running blood in the names of my fathers who have waited 'neath the altar of the Lord for their redemption![27] Go forth and worship in my name as it is written upon the gate."[28]

I am driven from the Aire and the Vision has grown dark. It is finished.

> August 31, 1975 E.V.
> 3:15 P.M. – 4:15 P.M.

---

[26] Again, פ = 80 = יסוד.
[27] The Magister Templi.
[28] I.e. NAKHEShT.

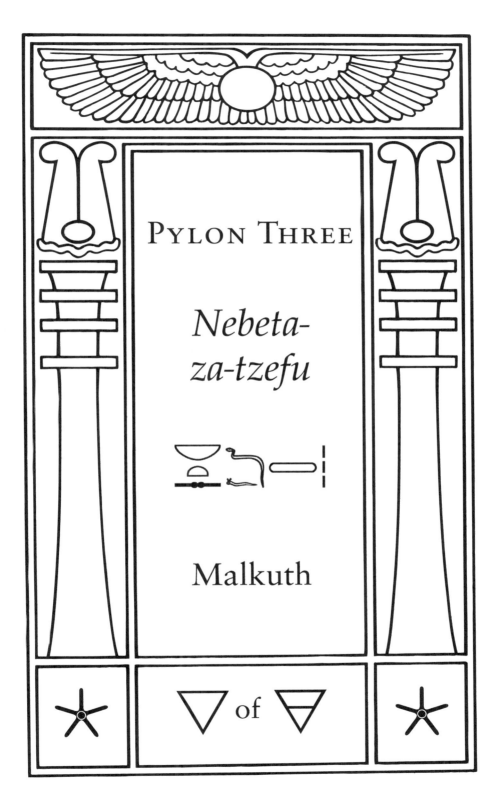

Harlequin, character in the commedia dell'arte of the 1670s, with batte or "slapstick," a magic wand used by the character to change the scenery of the play.

*A*s I enter the Pylon, I am assailed by a barrage of symbols whirling in a vortex that echoes out from the center of the Pylon. There is an image of ☿ and then the letter ב which is the reflection of 8.[1] Now I see a huge figure like a harlequin, yet I know him to be a Magus. He confounds the spheres with his laughter which is the Veil of the Eternal Spinner. Across the Aire there is a huge spider web and within each facet there are words and numbers, all individual and apart, yet penetrating the whole of the Vision.[2] Now I hear a voice:

> "There are nine entrances to this Pylon, each guarded by the Serpents of the Staff entwined about the Pillars of the Universe.[3] Yet thou shalt not entertain conversation with the Master of the Stone for he goeth solitary to seed the worlds. He is locked within his cape and cowl, which is called Yod, the tenfold Fire and Flame whereby our Mother is revealed.[4] Dust off thy feet and walk silent through the gates, for thereby dwell the gods, and thou art verily a god of a god of a god."[5]

I walk between two upright pillars of gleaming white and

---

[1] All Mercurial images, reflected into the Sephira Hod and from there into Water of Malkuth.
[2] The Magus is the master of Illusion. In Hindu mythology, माया *māyā* (illusion) is symbolized by a spider spinning a web.
[3] Here the Voice is instructing me that the Pylon in fact is connected to numerous gateways or bridges through spacetime. At the time, I missed this entirely.
[4] "The Hermit," Atu IX (♍ ruled by ☿). The Cowl of his Robe suggests Yod. Cf. "The Hermit" from the Tarot card design by Paul Foster Case.
[5] The word "god" three times = אל + אל + אל = 93.

now the Aire is opened unto me. I ask aloud for the name of the Pylon and I hear the words:

ECCLESIASTIQUE SUMMAE.[6]

Now an Angel appears and says:

"Thou who hast asked for the Word of the Pylon, knowest thou not that *thou* art verily the word itself which is but the seed of the ibis? Thou who dost seek the silvery minnow in the waters of the deep, yet doth not know the fish is dead?[7] ΙΧΘΥΣ[8] is swallowed whole by the birds of prey and impaled on the spikes.[9] Hath not the head of the Bull

---

[6] Latin, "The Highest Assembly." This Name is due to a reflection of Beth, the Magus who serves at the pleasure of the Highest Assembly, that is, the Supreme Chiefs of A∴A∴. This is not the name of this Pylon, but merely a pale reflection.

[7] Here, the "silver minnow" is an Archetypal symbol of the Self, cold-blooded and chthonic, hidden in the depths of the Unconscious as the "one fish" (μόνον ιχθύν), small and insignificant in size, and thus difficult to find. The silver coloration of the fish indicates its lunar and mercurial character, fleeting and rare. The Angel is stating that all of my Christian complexes had not yet been resolved; that while I sought the μόνον ιχθύν (the Self) I had not yet fully comprehended the falseness inherent in ιχθύς, the doctrines of the Christian Messiah.

[8] The word ΙΧΘΥΣ, "fish," is the familiar anagram for ΙΗΣΟΥΣ ΧΡΙΣΤΟΣ ΘΕΟΣ ΥΙΟΣ ΣΩΤΗΡ, "Jesus Christ, Son of God, Savior."

[9] This reference seems to have an analogy with the predatory birds such as shrikes and butcher birds, who impale their prey on thorns and spikes for later consumption. One of the benefits of this behavior of impaling insects is an apparent evolutionary adaptation of the shrike which allows consumption of the toxic lubber grasshopper (*Romalea guttata*). After waiting for a day or two for the toxins to degrade, the bird returns and eats the insect. There may be wisdom here that relates to a method for resolving one's upbringing in a Christian environment, if it so applies.

Atu I: The Magus — Thoth Tarot

been taken to appease the thirst of the Lady of the Sea?[10] Thou hast come from the House of the Lesser Mother in search of the Caduceus."

I am driven into a darkness that is the darkness of the soul. I seek to drive it away by uttering "Yod," so that the formless fire may deliver me and so that by virtue of the great flame Qadosh[11] the blackness may be dispersed. But I am confronted by an Angel dressed in a flaming orange gown. And upon the hem of his garments I see characters and runes in a velvet blue color.[12] He speaks:

> "Thou who hast entertained the Lord of the 15 passions and 15 vices[13] and the 80 motions[14] which are but the circumambulations of the Temple of Menthu,[15] heed the call of this Aire which is also diverse in 15 ways. Thou who hast seen the Lord traverse the sky and hast ques-

---

[10] This refers to a sacrificial rite that was a remnant from the Æon of Isis. Herodotus, in the Second Book of his *Histories*, relates how the Egyptians sacrificed a sacred bull, beheaded it, and cast the head into the river in honor of Isis. In this dialogue, the Angel indicates that I had yet to fully comprehend that the rituals of blood sacrifice are abrogate, remnants of the Æons of the Father (ΙΧΘΥΣ) and the Mother ("Lady of the Sea").

[11] Hebrew קדש "holy." See *Liber DCCCXIII*, Chapter VII.

[12] The colors orange and blue (opposite of orange in the color spectrum) are attributed to Hod in the Queen scale.

[13] Fifteen is the numeration of Hod הוד which is reflected into Water of Earth.

[14] Here, 80 signifies 8 × 10, Hod reflected into the water quadrant of Malkuth.

[15] The reference to the god Menthu is obscure. However, in Egyptian, the name Menthu means "nomad," which may be related to the concept of motion here. Many years later, I noted that the name Menthu spelled in Hebrew מנתו = 496, the number of Malkuth.

Menthu

tioned the Hammer of Thor which he bore instead of a staff. Seek thou the mystery of The Lovers. Would it vary if it were the Jawbone of an Ass?[16] Verily not, for the blood

---

[16] This is a reference to a dream I previously had on the night of Tuesday, March 25, 1975 E.V., wherein I beheld Mercury striding through the sky bearing the Hammer of Thor rather than the Caduceus. I did not understand the meaning of the Hammer. Upon reviewing *The Book of Thoth* after this vision, I was struck by Crowley's description of the child Cain holding the Hammer of Thor, wet with the blood of his brother. I had no conscious recollection of this passage. Furthermore, I did not understand the reference to the "Jawbone of an Ass." Later, I would discover it referred to the Book of Judges, Chapter 15, wherein

Samson slays a thousand Philistines with the jawbone of an ass (Z. Scheckel, 1860).

is spilled, not to glut the ravaging goddess but to build the Palace of the Rose."

Afar off in the background I hear the cry אל. And this is followed by another cry, יהוה אלוה ודעת. I understand this to be the Hermit transmitting the essence of Jupiter to the House of the Sun.[17] Turning my attention again to the Angel, I ask: "Yet, is it not a lie to think upon that death?"

Samson used the Jawbone of an Ass to slay a thousand men. Anciently, it was also believed that Cain used a jawbone to slay Abel (E.g., *The Holkham Bible Picture Book*, pl. 80. The Holkham Bible dates prior to 1350 E.V.). The message here is that it is not the weapon itself that is significant, but the purpose for which it is used.

[17] The word אל is attributed to Chesed (♃), and יהוה אלוה ודעת is the

He answers:

"Hath not the 81 been expanded to the Hawk-headed Lord of Strength and Silence? Is the number now not 93?
 Are the Trinity of Fathers not given over to the ways of the hermaphrodite?[18] Is not Thoth King *and* Queen?"[19]

And I asked him, "How is it you speak of IAO? For this is not the Mountain of Abiegnus which harbors the slain god."[20]
The Angel replied:

"Verily so, but herein are the splendrous waters which are fed by the wounds of the Hanged One who is suspended from the womb of the goddess. Is His name not IAO? Thou must pass the way of the Warlord to the Vision of Beauty. Is he not the god of bloodshed which is but the Bride of IAO?"

I said, "Thou wouldst snare me in the web of the Master of Illusion would I bid thee so!"[21]
He replied:

---

god name attributed to Tiphereth (☉). "The Hermit" (י) unites these Sephiroth. This is an example of the Ruach intruding on the Vision and bringing forth memorized correspondences.

[18] The formula of יאו = IAO = 81 to ויאעו = VIAOV = 93. See *Book IV*, Part III, Chapter 5.

[19] That is, Thoth = י = 10 = Malkuth (Queen). Yod spelled in full = יוד = 20 = כ = ♃ (King).

[20] At the time of this Vision, I did not know that the coming of the New Æon had transfigured the Mountain of Abiegnus from Tiphereth to Binah. See *Initiation in the Æon of the Child*, pp. 155–157.

[21] I was being tested. I had mistaken the Pylon for Hod, hence the Angel's reference to the Paths of נ ("The Hanged Man") and פ which leads to Netzach where the Vision of Beauty is attributed. I sensed this and balked at the attributions.

"Nay, but I would expose the adultery of the Twins who are ruled by this House. For they are but 12 and thus they are brought to thee so that the number may equal the Word of the Law and thus prevent thee from falling away from the Sun."[22]

Suddenly, I am battered and assailed by all manner of words, numbers and sounds, and all is lost in confusion! Yet, it seems to whirl now in a perfect pattern about me like a mosaic. I now see a god advance who bears a wand that is like an orb mounted with a crescent.[23] He is uttering a strange tongue and the symbols leap and fall into patterns with his words. Seeing this, I am bewildered and feel a great division in myself. My thoughts are lost to the "I" that is not "I," but "I" know not which, or whence or whither! "I" am not "I"!

But now a beautiful maiden embraces me and lifts me up and I see the entire Aire is of a gleaming silver, so bright that I cannot look upon it.

She speaks to me:

"It is well. Go forth and return to thy place, for thou hast understood the Mystery of the Aire, thou who art 12 and 6 and 3 and 1 and NONE."[24]

I said, "How can 'I' return, for 'I' am None?"
But she replied:

---

[22] This refers to the reflection of Hod, and Mercury which rules Gemini. The Twins = Vau spelled in full = וו = 12. The addition of 12 to 81 = 93, another reference to VIAOV ויאוע.

[23] Suggestive of the sign of ☿ Mercury.

[24] I did not intellectually understand this Aire for a long time. The numerical cipher remains unclear.

"Nay, *No Man* is None, but thou art Two which shall be brought to Nought."[25]

Now I am torn into pieces that are the atoms that are in turn the stars of the Universe. It seems that all is lost to the eternal fragmentation.[26]

But I hear the words:

"The Hammer IS the Staff of Construction!"[27]

The Aire is slammed shut like a door.
The entity K.N. is back.[28]

> November 12, 1975 E.V.
> 10:30 P.M. – 11:30 P.M.

---

[25] "No Man" refers to The Magister Templi. I was being reminded that I still dwelled in the world of duality below the Abyss.

[26] The Ruach is incapable of organizing non-linear data, and thus all appears disorganized. This is illusion.

[27] The reference is to the Hammer of Thor held by Mercury. I learned later that the function of the Supreme and Third Order is Construction while the nature of the Outer Order is Destruction.

[28] The initials K.N. are my motto initials as a member of the Outer College.

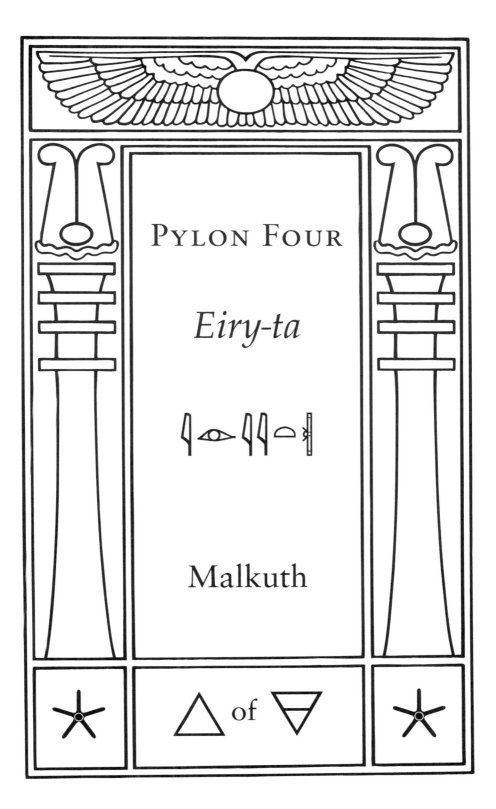

I AM WALKING DOWN a long hallway. On either side many entities stand, each holding a staff surmounted with a large feather. The staffs give the appearance of being fans, yet I know them to be the emblem of MAAT.¹

This hallway goes as far as I can see.

Now I approach the end of the hallway and there is a large green throne flanked with two great urns. The throne is empty and behind it there is a large curtain decorated with fleurs-de-lys. No sound is uttered. The hall is in complete silence.

But words are placed within my mind though not spoken. I perceive that this throne is an image of the Pylon.

Now words arise: "It is NOT the Dais."²

I begin to see an image of a goddess upon the throne. She is transparent and I am able to see through her. There is a vision beyond her that seems to be a golden desert adorned with pyramids. She bares her breast to me and I see upon it the Seal of the Holy Order and the markings of our Holy Lady Babalon.

She has become tangible and I see that she does not look upon my face but beyond, as if in a trance. Between her legs I see a great sword that is embedded in the base of the green stone. There is a writing upon the blade.

It is the word ΘΕΛΗΜΑ. The sword looks very much like the Ace of Swords as it is given in the Tarot.

Suddenly, there is a great clap of thunder that strikes me to the ground.

I hear a horrible grinding sound like marble or granite being rent asunder! From behind the throne a huge beast rises. It has

---

¹ The emblem of MAAT is the ostrich feather ß.

² The Dais is attributed to Jupiter. This admonition was to remind me not to confuse the planes, as I had once confounded certain symbolism of Netzach with Chesed.

Ace of Swords — Thoth Tarot

Amemut the devourer of souls

the head of a crocodile, the feet of a lion and the body of some gray thing.[3] This beast is dreadful to look upon and terrible to hear, for it roars a hideous roar that fills the hall with the breath of its nostrils! Its jaws are crashing together—this is the source of the thunder! Between its teeth I see what appears to be men and women who cling to the teeth so as not to be lost. Yet, they *are* lost for they are the shells of the devoured and there is no life in them.

The Priestess upon the throne[4] holds out her hand now and I see the image of a heart, like the Egyptian hieroglyph *ib* (♡). I cannot tell if it is an image or whether it is *my* heart that she holds. I think the latter is true and this is indeed my very heart. She raises her right hand now and the beast is silenced. It sinks down behind the throne and I see it no more.

The Priestess begins to speak:

---

[3] The "gray thing" was the body of a hippopotamus. This is 🝃𓃥𓃡𓂋𓃠, *ʿm-mwt*, Amemut, the devourer of the dead in the Hall of Truth.

[4] Earlier in the Vision, she is called "the goddess." Now, without explanation, she is called "The Priestess." This was due to an unconscious association I made with Atu II, "The High Priestess."

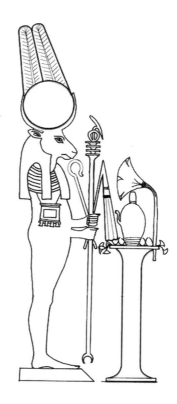

"Pour out the Vial upon the waters, that the Fire of my Father may be loosed upon the worlds and burn up the iniquities of men in the blaze of his wrath. O Great One! Quench thy thirst and eat them up with Glory as it is written![5] Can the Bull stand not upon the four-square altar and bring forth the Sword of Justice? Thou art given over to the ways of the whoremonger and the bastions of the Aire are shattered and fall like weakened ivory. The heart is entwined by the Serpent of the Tree. All is lost! All is lost! All is lost![6] Woe, yea woe! For the daughter is lost to the gaze of the seeker!"

---

[5] Perhaps a reference to *Liber CCXX*, II:14.

[6] Frater Adjuvo suggested to me that "lost" = לוסת = "Lust." Note that לוסת = 496, the number of Malkuth in full.

I see a bull-man approach, clad only in a great cape. He grasps the goddess with furious arms and begins to ravage her! They struggle in the throes of their lust, again and again.[7] Now, a great wind arises and blows about them as they are lost in the fight of the passions.

The Aire is rent asunder and I witness the force of its might.

The curtain is blown aside and I am permitted to see past the throne and beyond the hall. I hear a Voice:

"Enter! For thou hast been weighed in the balances and thine heart hath been found worthy of the MAAT feather. Amemut is denied! The devourer hath ceased! The roarings have subsided and the Equilibrium is restored."

I walk through the space between the curtains and I come upon a new Vision.[8] It is like flowers, but this is not correct. I cannot describe the smell and I am unsure if I am using the sense of smell or whether the awareness of sweetness is perceived by some other means.

An entity approaches and he is singing a chant:

> "The living flame upon the brow
>   of Hut-Hooru[9] is open!
> The sword hath cleaved the offered spices!
>   Give goats, oxen, geese with plenty!
> Bountiful blessings upon the Child!"

He sings so sweetly that I am touched by the Hymn that he utters and I seek to sing with him. But now I see him clearly and

---

[7] Cf. the myth of Europa, ravished by Zeus in the form of a bull. ☽ is exalted in ♉, ruled by ♀. These are but reflections of an aspect of Netzach.

[8] Here is the entrance through a secret Pylon that leads to Netzach.

[9] I.e., Hathor, 𓉡 Ḥwt Ḥr.

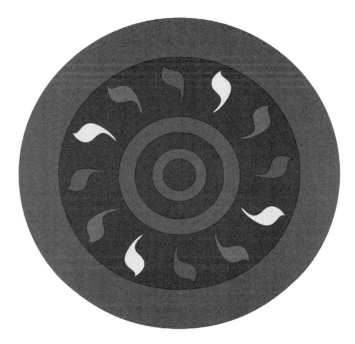

The Angelic Sigil of Fire. (See color plate following page 144.)

note that he is a most terrible being to look upon. His face is handsome like a Greek god, but his eyes are entirely black, like carved obsidian. There is no white about them, only a piercing blackness that knows the depths of my soul!

He is placing offerings upon a sacrificial stone. Upon the stone there is an emblem engraved.

It is the Angelic Sigil of Fire and it is in a vivid red and green color.

I speak to him, "Give unto me the mystery of this Pylon so that I may come to know the attractions and repulsions of my own being, that I may come to know the balance of myself."[10]

He looks at me deeply, but only turns away.

As he departs he sings:

---

[10] The Task of the Philosophus of the A∴A∴

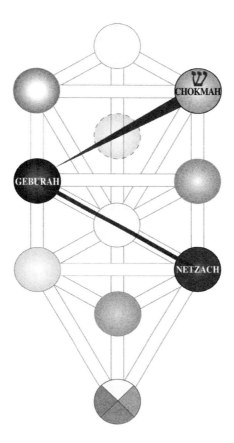

The reflection of Fire from Chokmah to Geburah to Netzach.

> "The Crown of Hut-Hooru is open
>   The Child shall come forth anew.
> The gift of Love is of the infant.
>   Rise guards! Rise winds!
> Blow through the tomb."

Although he continues to sing, I cannot hear any more for he is far away. I look again to the altar and notice that it is like the altar that is upon the stélé of revealing, only much wider. I am puzzled as to the nature of the gifts.

Suddenly, there is the sound of a rushing wind. I look up and see a great flame descend from the sky, strike the altar and consume it utterly! There is also now a legion of Angels in the air and they sing a new song in a beautiful chorus that is impossible to describe! I am moved by the beauty of the song! Their glory is of gleaming white and golden raiment which streams forth from the throne of the Most High!

I hear a Voice:

"Hath not the Fire of our Father licked up the offerings upon the stone? Yea, that Fire that darts and flashes through the hidden depths of the Universe[11] which is but the womb of Our Lady Nuit, the goddess of the Infinite Stars. Is not the Flame reflected even from the Wisdom unto the Strength and even unto the Victorious Palace?[12] Mighty, mighty, mighty is He who that decreed the observation of times and seasons!"[13]

Now I see an Angel who bears a golden vial and he pours it out upon the blackened stone that was the offering table. The fluid is of an emerald green that sparkles with flecks of golden red. As it spills upon the stone, lotus blossoms rise and bloom with great beauty.

Another Angel cries:

"Who hath decreed that the waters should be wormwood

---

[11] Cf. *The Chaldean Oracles*, Westcott ed., 199: "When thou shalt behold that holy and formless Fire shining flashingly through the depths of the Universe: Hear thou the Voice of Fire."

[12] Fire is reflected from Chokmah (Wisdom) to Geburah (Strength) and then to Netzach (the Victorious Palace). See diagram on page 77.

[13] Among the Egyptians, the god Tahuti was He who regulated the times and seasons. He is the Word, the Magus, and hence Chokmah.

to poison the bowels of the sea?[14] Woe, yea woe unto the rivers and streams that would deny the Flame of the Vault![15] Woe, yea woe to the stone that would deny the

---

[14] Cf. Revelation 8:10–11. However, see *Initiation in the Æon of the Child*, Chapter 8. The Star Wormwood that fell to Earth has begun to poison the waters (the Unconscious of men) with dis-ease, the leaven of transformation.

[15] I.e., the Formless Flame that moves through the Vault of heaven. Cf. *The Chaldean Oracles*, Westcott ed., 196: "If thou often invokest thou shalt see all things growing dark; and then when no longer is visible unto thee the High-arched Vault of Heaven, when the Stars have lost their Light and the Lamp of the Moon is veiled, the Earth abideth not,

kiss of the Flaming Child!¹⁶ Is this not the place of the Cross surmounted with the Kteis? Doth the Palace not encompass the Tree?¹⁷ Verily it is so! It is so! Cry forth, o children! The time is come, is come, when no man may seek safety beneath the stones and mountains! No stone may be left unturned lest the College be profaned! Divest thyself of thine ornaments who would call forth the Golden God of the West!"¹⁸

And yet another Angel cries:

"Come forth, O ye Mysteries of Creation that the Word be fulfilled! Open yourselves and declare the triumph of

---

and around thee darts the Lightning Flame and all things appear amid thunders."

¹⁶ The Formless Fire is here called "the Child." Cf. *The Chaldean Oracles*, Westcott ed., 198: "A similar Fire flashingly extending through the rushings of Air, or a Fire formless whence cometh the Image of a Voice, or even a flashing Light abounding, revolving, whirling forth, crying aloud. Also there is the vision of the fire-flashing Courser of Light, or also a Child, borne aloft on the shoulders of the Celestial Steed, fiery, or clothed with gold, or naked, or shooting with the bow shafts of Light, and standing on the shoulders of the horse; then if thy meditation prolongeth itself, thou shalt unite all these Symbols into the Form of a Lion." The practical instruction is that those who would seek Initiation must submit themselves to the transformative power. In the beginning, this is normally disquieting and painful. But these sorrows are but shadows that pass away, and with Initiation comes the dispersal of the illusion. See *Liber LXV*, V:1–10.

¹⁷ The symbol of Venus ♀ (the Cross surmounted by the Kteis) projected upon the Tree of Life connects all of the Sephiroth, representing the whole of Life embraced by Nature (Isis).

¹⁸ The symbolic password to the Grade of Neophyte is נה "ornament," which has a value of 55 = Σ(1–10), the Mystic number of Malkuth. The "Golden God of the West" here refers to the Holy Guardian Angel. Cf. *Liber VII*, IV:58 and *Liber CCXX*, III:31.

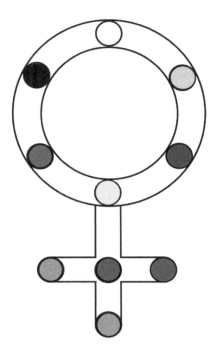

The Astrological Sign of Venus projected on the Tree of Life.

O madâ-i[19] that the prophecies be declared which are the pages of thy dreams!
 Devour us, o ye through-thrusting Fire![20]
 Ō go go madâ-a anatahèrètzâ quo babalanuda tèu razamahè tutulu!"[21]

---

[19] ⌐ ƐϿƆϿ⌐ (Enochian), "the Five Gods." This refers to the Lords or Rulers of the five elements.

[20] "through-thrusting fire" is a translation of the Enochian ⌐Ͽ ƐϿBⱯƐႦ ta malapereji. See The First Key of the Calls of the Thirty Æthyrs.

[21] ⌐ Ⴆ⌐ Ⴆ⌐ ƐϿϽ ϿⱯϿƐϿF ЩЩ VϿVϿCⱯϿϿ Ɐᴚ ƐPϿƐϿƠ ⱯᴚⱯᴚᴚ (Enochian). "The five cry out, cry out, thy god is as a burning coal or a harlot who fixeth her eyes upon one who shall attain." The Angel instructed me that the key to my aspiration is the Holy Guardian Angel who is likened unto a "burning coal" (cf. *Liber LXV*, V:9), and later in

They all sing together in a tongue so sweet that I cannot utter the magnificence of its refrain! And I seek to look upon them but I cannot face the Vision, for a golden sun streams forth from behind the choir of Angels. The rays are like Yods and Arrows and great winds of strength!

I cannot describe the nature of the Vision!

I am swept into a divine bliss that is as sweet as honey and bathes me in the essence of essences!

(Here a lapse of several minutes occurred, of which no memory was retained.)[22]

Though I try to remain in this palace of wonder, the singing fades away and the Vision passes from me, leaving me huddled in my *āsana*. All is again silent and I am alone upon the sand.[23]

Suddenly, I feel a jolt and I am back into the body.

Yet, the beauty of the Vision still lingers and I dwell in the majesty of its memory. But the memory is imperfect and impure as the words are imperfect and impure, and cannot give witness to the things I have seen.

Selah.[24]

November 14, 1975 E.V.
1:00 P.M. – 2:00 P.M.

Babalon who is the Guardian of the Abyss unto whom I must eventually give all.

[22] A *samādhi* was experienced here.

[23] Note that no mention was ever made of being on the sand until after the *samādhi*.

[24] Hebrew, סלה, which signifies the end of a musical passage or Psalm. I uttered the word spontaneously.

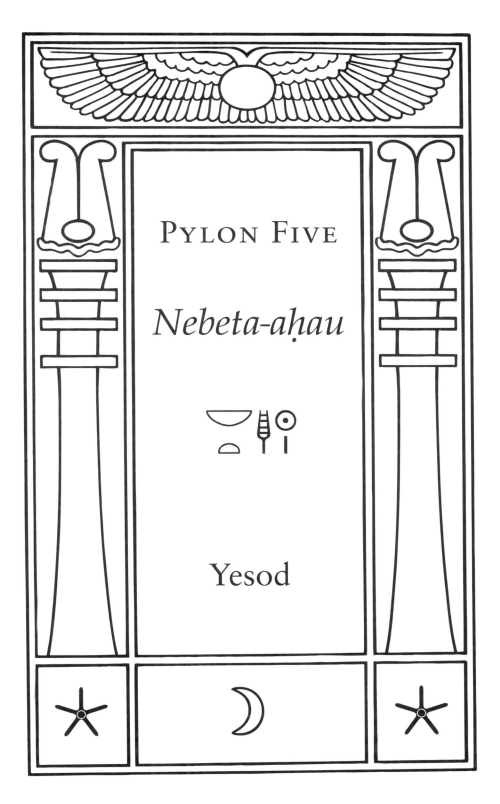

The Sign of Shu

*S*TARS AND GALAXIES ARE STREAMING past me. I seem to be traveling through vast space. It is possible that I am the moving object and they are unmoving. It is no matter for the movement occurs or *seems* to occur and this is the iniquity of the ages.[1]

(Yet, therein is found the foundation of all truth, or truth as I perceive it.)

Now I approach the Pylon. It is like a *vesica piscis* with blinding silver rays of light streaming forth. I hear what seems to be a choir of Angels singing—this pertains to the mystery of Air. Now there is an Angel at the Gate who steps in my path. His countenance is fierce and demands to see the Sign of passing. I show him the Sign of Shu with his hands upon the arched body of our Lady of the Stars, Nuit.

He speaks:

"Pass by, o iniquitous Son of Earth. The Sign is sure and exact and the breath of life flows in thy veins. For it is the air that uplifts the vault from the ripened earth lest the flowers be trampled."[2]

I say, "Bring unto me the guardian of the Pylon so that its mystery may be divulged."

He replies, folding his great wings across his breast:

"Verily, I am the guardian of this place, the watch guard of the treasure of the Stone, the Serpent-One who rises

---

[1] Motion about a point is iniquity. The *Rashith Ha Gilgalim* or Whirling First Motion was the first appearance of iniquity, or imperfection. The "foundation" (Yesod) of truth below the Abyss is that Change = Stability ($2° = 9°$).

[2] Cf. *Liber CCXX*, I:26.

against the impious ones, the sons of Earth who would pry open the Sanctuary and pass water in the livid pool and who would scorn the sacred mysteries."[3]

I say unto him, "Take me unto the abode. Divulge unto me the mystery of the Aire so that I may be firm."
The Angel draws a great sword and says:

"So be it! Do what thou wilt shall be the whole of the Law."

I reply to him, "Love is the law, love under will."
Immediately, there are swift winds rising. They are not wild and untamed but flowing with sweetness and strength.
The Angel points upward:

"Rise up unto the Sanctuary of the Lady. (Here, I see or hear the word ΣΕΛΗΝΗ.[4]) Follow me and keep close lest the dispersion vex thee and dispel the Vision."[5]

I look upward and I see the true Pylon looming skyward. It is very beautiful but I fear that I cannot rise with the Angel and enter this gateway of glory.
But he says:

---

[3] His name is 𓏞𓀀𓏤𓂝𓏛𓌳 *Seta-ma-eiri-fa,* which means "Burns with his Eye."

[4] Greek, *Selene,* Greek goddess of the Moon.

[5] This is a warning that I should have noted more carefully. I was vexed by dispersion throughout this Vision, as I had been since I entered the Pylon. My own intellectual faculty continually intruded and lying spirits went undetected. This Vision is most unsatisfactory on a number of counts. At the time of the Vision, the moon was waning. It was not the optimum time for the operation.

"Fear not and be not troubled. For I will carry thee up. I will bear thee up in the strength of thine Oath."

It is suddenly clear to me that this alone will open the Pylon, if the Oath be taken in all truth. And now I am in the archway of the Pylon. There are characters written on each side. The Pylon is immense in size and built of gray stone that gleams with a strange purity. I try to read the inscriptions.

They are in hieroglyphics:

(I tried to dictate to the Scribe a few of the hieroglyphs that he can see upon the Pylon. This proved to be very difficult and time-consuming.)

This is all I can read.[6] It is part of that which is written on the right side of the Pylon. I wish to read the left side but the Angel takes my arm and says:

"Come. The Mass is in celebration and it is allowed for your witness."

---

[6] The hieroglyphs are only fragments of what was actually seen. The lacunae marks indicate missing characters. I dictated the hieroglyphs quickly, trying to capture a few hoping to translate it later. This was unsuccessful, as not enough were dictated to give a clue to the text. The initial characters 𓉐𓅱 *ḥw* are the first letters of an unknown longer word. 𓆓 *ḏd mdw* means "words spoken" and usually precedes a speech, here missing. The characters 𓂓𓍑𓏛 most certainly spell the word 𓂓𓍑𓏛𓆑 *nft*, "breath." The word 𓎛𓎛 *ḥḥ*, means "millions," while the sun disc 𓇳 is an isolated, unconnected determinitive. 𓇋𓂝𓎛 is almost complete. The full word is without doubt 𓇋𓂝𓎛 *iʿ*, "moon." While there are words that are indicative of the attributions of Luna and Air, it is impossible to determine a meaningful sentence from the fragments.

I hear a chant that seems to be coming from a great banquet table. There is a large group of entities and goddesses praising and drinking and holding aloft their cups. They are singing:

"A qa dua, tu-f ur bayu, ba'a bayu, du du ner-af an nuteru."[7]

I understand that there is more contained therein than the profane understand. I press unto the Angel who is with me and say, "Is it so that within the frame of this cry there are great secrets?"

He replies:

"It is so. Blessed is he who hath heard the secret call of the hidden sword. And this sword verily is a Book, and with such a weapon will the Order be pushed and brought forth as it is written."[8]

And now I hear what sounds like deep lamentation and weeping.

The Angel says:

"Fear not, for it is only the weeping of the Eagle to make

---

[7] The chant from the stélé of revealing but with one significant change. 𓇋 𓂓 𓇼𓇼 𓏏𓅱𓆑 𓅨𓂋 𓃀𓂋𓏤𓏪 𓃀𓂋 𓉻 𓃀𓂋𓏤𓏪 *i k3 dw3 tw.f wr b3w b3 ꜥ3 b3w ddw nrw.f n nṯrw*, "O exalted one, may he be praised, the great one of Spirits, Great Spirit of Spirits, who gives the fear of himself to the gods." The Vision gives *b3 ꜥ3 b3w* "Great Spirit of Spirits" where the stélé has *b3 ꜥ3 šfyt* "Great Spirit of dignity" (Crowley gives the last word as *Chefu* based on the now-outdated Boulaq Museum transliteration of 𓍱 *šfyt shefyet*, as *chefu*. See *The Holy Books of Thelema*, pp. 243 and 256.)

[8] Cf. *Liber CCXX*, III:38.

way for the passing of the Cube. Lo! Is she not ever a moon? And unto her is not given the stooping starlight?"[9]

I bow my head, for I am witness to the sanctity of the rite.

Now, all is silent. There is no sound at all. It is as if the whole of the Aire were caught up in the holiness of the offering.

However, I see a most beautiful goddess approach. She is of a great size, and wears a gown without sleeves. It is a shimmering blue color.

She holds out her hand and says:

"Come unto *me!*"

Immediately, I am aware of the evils that are reflected in this place.[10] At once I trace the Banishing Pentagram of Air.[11] She contorts into a hideous grinning creature that vanishes before me. I see that she was but a reflection of the Abyss.[12]

Looking upward again, I see a deep blue voluptuous sky studded with stars. And now I hear the true resounding cry:

"Come unto *me!*"[13]

I am humbled and say, "I would come unto thee, but I am stained and unworthy."

---

[9] Eagle + Cube = ◯ + ☐ = Squaring the Circle = ΚΤΕΙΣ + ΦΑΛΛΟΣ = ☽ + ☉ = ☉ etc.

[10] Correction: they are not "reflected" here. They *abide* there as they do in the old gray land, or any place below the Abyss.

[11] Thereby intended to banish all things *except* those of an Airy nature.

[12] Again, incorrect. This dog-faced demon was not a reflection of the Abyss, but merely a lying Astral spirit.

[13] This voice came from my intellect which was intruding and trying to restore control. It did not have objective reality.

The Voice says:

"I will make thee clean. There is no bond that can unite the divided but love."[14]

The Angel beside me speaks and says:

"It is well. Thou didst pass the ordeal of the hideous one. Many are they who fall on account of the beauty of the Mighty Devil.[15] Those who seek the mockers among the tombs do not perceive the Devils in the midst of the Sanctuary. Was it not said, 'Rid thyself of thine ornaments who would call the god?'"[16]

Once again, I see the Aire most clearly, but it cannot be described with clarity. There are many palaces here, each transposing one with the other at such a great rate of speed that I cannot perceive their distinction. Yet I know that they remain distinct. The interaction of the palaces is the dance of wonder that insures the strength of the firmament. The Angel says:

"Herein is a great mystery. For this is that of which it is written: And God said, let there be a firmament in the midst of the waters.[17] For the firmament is of the Yod which is the first letter of the Name of the Aire and doth unite the Waters which are 80, the number of the

---

[14] Again, an intellectual intrusion by myself.

[15] All representations of dishonesty and falsehood are aspects of Choronzon. They were anciently called 𓇋𓊃𓆑𓏏 *isft*, "wrong-doing" or "chaos." They stand in contradistinction to those things which are part of Maat 𓐙𓂝𓏏𓏤 *mꜣꜥt*, "truth" or "order."

[16] Personal weaknesses lurk not only in the outermost dark places of our soul, but often in places of light. Cf. *Liber LXV*, III:5–12.

[17] Genesis 1:6.

Sephira.[18] The firmament is concealed in the midst as the ΦΑΛΛΟΣ is concealed in the womb of the lady of the moon. For she is the Virgin as he that doth conceal it. Those who would rebuke these mysteries are outcast and forlorn in the wasteland."[19]

I am permitted to see the depth of this mystery.[20] Yet, I say unto the Angel, "Have I beheld all of the mysteries here? Hold it from me not, I pray thee, for I seek to equate the 2 with the 9 in all its perfection."
The Angel replies:

"Herein, the 2 cannot be equated perfectly with the 9 but only after another manner. Therein is the Law of *He Who Utters*. This is the place of the bow, she the huntress who fits the arrow for the heart of the lion."[21]

I ask the Angel if "He Who Utters" is the Magus who creates by Speech. He replies:

"Verily, my child. Is it not so that Tahuti is the One Who Utters? Is it not so that he was the god of the moon among the people of the Black Land?[22] Seek the equivalence of

---

[18] The letter י is the first letter of Yesod יסוד and also is the central letter in מים, "water," where the letter מ (40) occurs twice = 80, the numeration of Yesod יסוד = 10 + 60 + 6 + 4 = 80.

[19] The Angel uttered this last sentence after I thought to myself, "This is just incredibly puerile!"

[20] I attempted to placate the Angel by saying this, but I still considered the previous speech to be extremely elementary; hence my next question.

[21] Diana the huntress. The lunar crescent ☽ is by shape the bow of Yesod. The Arrow is ♐ fired into the Heart (Tiphereth).

[22] The Black Land is 𓆎𓏏𓊖 *kmt* Egypt. Tahuti is 𓅝𓏤 *dḥwty*, "Thoth," who as the God of magic and writing is the Magus. He was also called

Tahuti

my words therein. Yet the Word and its mate may not be perceived by the skill of number and of the Book, for this leads to the House of Mercury. Seek the unity of the diverse with the equation."[23]

𓇋𓎛𓃀𓅝𓏤, *Iḥ dḥwty*, Tahuti the moon god, the God of measurement.

[23] The Word (Chokmah) and its mate (Binah) cannot be Understood by use of Qabalah or Tarot ("the skill of number or of the Book"). These are both of the nature of ☿ (Hod). The perfect unity is only to be found in the equation $9° = 2°$, not $2° = 9°$.

Khonsu

The Angel begins to change his appearance before my eyes, flashing back and forth, to and fro, from image to image. First, a smiling god, then a skeleton.[24] Everything about me changes and conforms to its opposite and yet continues to retain coherency.

A Voice cries out:

"Return! Return! KHONSU has fled unto the outermost

---

[24] Perhaps the smiling god is א ("The Fool"), and the skeleton is ♄ ("The Universe"), polar opposites in the Tarot cards, the "First and Last."

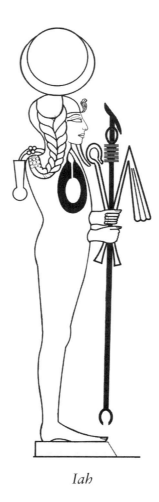

Iah

regions, even unto the Abyss of Hell. OOHA[25] has folded his head beneath his wing. ISU[26] rejoices in the known, suffering the delights of the inflicted wounds pouring forth

---

[25] From Coptic ⲟⲟϩ < Egyptian 𓇋𓂝𓎛 *i͗ḥ*, "moon." The reference is to 𓇋𓂝𓎛𓅝 *i͗ḥ ḏḥwty*, Tahuti the moon god, or simply *Iah* the god of the moon.

[26] This is uncertain, but possibly intended to refer to Asi, "Isis," or else it is corrupt.

from the spear of the Lord. Return! Return! And recite the praise of the ever-flowing, ever-fluid, ever-holy Lady."

Now, once again I see the great banquet table with the congregation of gods and angels. They all stand erect and give the sign of Shu. The Angel at my side also gives the Sign. I face the deities and return the Sign. I now hear the clashing of great cymbals. They ring nine times, each one fading more than the one previous. The last is so faint that I can hardly hear it.

The Vision is no more.

Sunday, May 16, 1976 E.V.
(time not recorded)[27]

---

[27] This was inexcusable.

I have gone past the *vesica piscis* which forms the outer gate of the Fifth Pylon.[1] I am now approaching the second gate. I give the Sign of Shu to the Guardian and I am granted immediate entrance. I pass into the midst of a great circular marketplace. It seems to be abandoned. There is no one in sight. In the silence I can hear the sound of my own footsteps. There are numerous streets and passageways leading out from the agora. It has the appearance of a maze. I call aloud, "Bring unto me the Guardian of this sphere."

Instantly, in the air above me I see an Angel with large wings wearing a light blue gown. She quickly descends, holding a shewstone in which there is a single flickering flame. She speaks:

"What deemest thou?"

I reply, "I come that I may forge my way to the central mystery of this Pylon."

She says:

"Many are they that have thought this, but few persevere. The way is dark and full of terrors. Those who would look upon the face of the Empty One must cling unto their Oath and not falter lest they be cast into the outermost regions of despair and torment."

---

[1] Eight months after my first attempt to explore the Fifth Pylon I attempted it again. I had grown increasingly dissatisfied with the initial results and was certain that my own intellect had marred the first attempt. I was determined to redeem myself and put a leash on the Ruach. It should be noted that I executed this second Scry after exploring the Sixth Pylon, but before the Seventh Pylon.

I answer her, "I am ready."

Then the Angel loses all form and becomes as a mist with a faint light in the center. I am bidden to walk into the center of the mist and pass through to the heart of the mystery. I do as I am commanded.

I have come upon a large chamber with a long passageway at the far end. It appears to be constructed of stone. On the right-hand side of the passageway there are six robed figures, all standing erect, silent and somber with hoods drawn.

The first is standing next to a wall torch. I walk past him and he says θάνατος.[2] The second is standing beside a torch upon a tripod. As I pass him he says ἔργον.[3] I continue to walk. The third says λήθιος.[4] The Fourth says ἥλιος.[5] With this, I try to think of the sun.

But this is wrong, for a Voice cries out:

"There is no light in the chasm of the tomb!"

The fifth figure is holding a bowl, within which is a flame. He says μνήμη.[6] The last is holding two spears, the points of which are flame. His word is ἅγιος.[7] They all speak at the same time, repeating their words over and over, yet each giving the illusion of separate speech.[8] Before me now I see a large black doorway.

---

[2] "Death" (θάνατος).

[3] "Work" (ἔργον).

[4] "Causing forgetfulness" (λήθιος).

[5] "The sun" (ἥλιος).

[6] "Memory" (μνήμη).

[7] "Holy" (ἅγιος).

[8] The initial letter of each of these Greek words = θελημα. These figures with their repeating speech represent personifications of the Ruach. My own ego autonomously attempted to establish control by creating organized data as it confronted a situation over which it would have no control at all, and one which could have led to disintegration of the ego-making faculty.

There is a sense of impending doom in the Aire. An indescribable stench issues forth from the opening.

All at once, an entity appears. He is wearing a black robe and full hood. He motions to the door and bellows:

"BEHOLD! THE DWELLER ON THE THRESHOLD!"[9]

[NOTE BY SCRIBE: At this point the Seer screamed and fell over. I could not see him, as he was seated behind me, but could hear that he was writhing on the floor of the Temple, whether from pain or fear I could not tell. He began to make inhuman gurgling sounds as if he were strangling, then began to heave and sob. Then followed approximately three minutes of complete silence, after which the Seer addressed me directly: "I couldn't begin to tell you this. It's like being plunged into a 'hell' of emotion. Then suddenly, it stops and all that is left is the Vision. No emotion or feeling *at all*. That thing is like a writhing mass of tentacles; all the foulness you can imagine. I'm still there." The Seer then resumed the Vision.]

---

[9] The term "Dweller on the Threshold" was the creation of Bulwer-Lytton in his novel *Zanoni* (1842). Theosophy adopted the term and from there it was incorporated by the Hermetic Order of the Golden Dawn. See *Liber LXV*, IV:33–37 for another description of this figure. There, one also finds the description of his stench, and he is described as "more hideous than the shells of Abaddon." אבדון, Prince of גשכלה, the Qliphoth of Chesed. Cf. also Revelation 9:1–11, where Abaddon is the Angel of the bottomless pit. His name in Greek is Apollyon, "destroyer." The Dweller on the Threshold has much in common with the "Shadow" of Jungian psychology (the negative aspects of the personality), but it is more than this. The Dweller on the Threshold represents the collective Evil of all of our previous lives and current incarnation. The occult tradition consistently affirms that each Initiate must confront this horror before we are granted access to the Holy of Holies. In its fullest sense, this is not experienced until the Initiation of the Babe of the Abyss. The experience described in this Vision is but the reflection of that horror in Yesod.

Now there is a beautiful woman, a goddess. She begins to speak:

"Was it not written that those who seek the mockers among the tombs do not perceive the devils in the midst of the Sanctuary?"

She transforms into a golden lynx, then into a python. It changes into a basilisk, then a camel, then a jackal, then into the Set animal. Lastly it changes into a little satyr.[10]

Now there is a tremendous Voice. It laughs aloud, saying:

"When the hairs of the beard of Arik Anpin[11] were befouled, there was I! When the sword of Zauir Anpin[12] was broken, there was I! When Malkah[13] was spat upon in the marketplace, there was I! When the sirens sing their songs and the sailors are lured to the rocks, there am I! Let those who would lift their hand unto the Smooth Point[14] beware, for in the midst of Joy I dwell!"

---

[10] This "beautiful woman" who displays all the transformations is none other than the Evil Persona, or the Dweller on the Threshold.

[11] אריך אנפין, the Macroprosopus or "Vast Countenance" (Kether). The beard of Macroprosopus is divided into 13 "dispositions" which open to the 13 gates of Mercy. It is written in *The Zohar*, "Those thirteen dispositions are found in the beard. And in proportion to the purity of his beard, according to its dispositions is a man said to be true; for also whosoever beholdeth his beard, that man is desirous of truth." (Cf. Mathers, *The Kabbalah Unveiled*, pp. 134–142, "Concerning the Beard of Macroprosopus.")

[12] זעיר אנפין, the Microprosopus or "Lesser Countenance." (The hexad of Sephiroth from Chesed–Yesod, centered in Tiphereth to which is referred the Sword.) Zauir Anpin is the son of the Ancient of Ancient Ones (Arik Anpin) and Prince and Bridegroom of Malkuth the Bride.

[13] מלכה "Queen," a name of Malkuth as the virgin Bride of Zauir Anpin.

[14] נקודה פשוטה a name of Kether. Cf. *Liber LXV*, I:9–10.

[I spoke to the Scribe and said, "Spell JOY like IOI in *The Book of Lies*."][15]

I say unto the Dweller, "Thou liest! There is no substance in thy words, for thou art a hollow mockery!"

He begins to babble in a different tongue. It sounded something like this:

"Reni reni gaga jipa kinewa teka teka fahjeh fahjeh pezo lek tak timina felelit."

I perceive that this is not a language at all, but an attempt to confuse.[16]

He speaks again:

"Are not all languages gibberish, having meaning only by the wit of them that spew it out?
    Let the virgins be beguiled by sweet songs of the lyre. Them will I flay and scatter to the winds. Let those who will, seek to climb the ladder of Set, for I will smite them in my fury, even as the rushing water battles the twigs that play upon its foam."[17]

He continues with incessant talking, of which I can only get about the tenth part.

There is only one way to succeed here. Therefore I assume the Sign of Hoor-paar-kraat.

He flies into a rage, screaming and stamping up and down.

---

[15] A purely intellectual interjection by myself to regain some sense of balance. I was thinking of chapter twelve of *The Book of Lies*, "Dragon-flies."

[16] It was glossolalia, not a language.

[17] Cf. *Liber LXV*, III:56.

I think of that which is written in the *Tao Te Ching*: "What stills muddy water? Silence."[18]

[NOTE BY SCRIBE: A period of silence ensued, lasting perhaps two to two and half minutes.]

I have just passed through a storm of Vision. Images swarmed around me. Faces and apparitions loomed up before me. The image of the Dweller on the Threshold doubled. Two faces appeared and began to blaspheme the silence, saying that all Visions were nonsense, that the Scribe was an idiot for writing it down, that all my words were lies and drivel. Once again I thought of the *Tao Te Ching*.

I then approached the Dweller and merged with his essence. Instantly, the storm ceased and its Visions passed away.[19]

I am now standing behind a broad table upon which rest several large waxen Seals. I cannot perceive the meaning of this.

As I am about to describe the Seals, an Angel appears and says:

"Stay thine hand and write not of these Seals. That which shall be loosed shall be loosed in good season."[20]

---

[18] This is a paraphrase of the *Tao Te Ching* XV, 3: "Who can clear muddy water? Stillness will accomplish this." (Crowley, *Tao Te Ching*, p. 30).

[19] This was a dangerous thing to do, and my Instructor was shocked when he learned of it. However, he congratulated me for having the courage to do it and the good fortune to survive it. Although it is vital to confront the negative aspects of our consciousness, to do in the manner demonstrated here is strongly discouraged.

[20] These Seals were inscribed in Enochian. The Scribe, Frater I.A.T.A., was very upset that I could not communicate what was etched upon these seals. But the Angel promised that they will be "loosed in good season." Who shall eventually loose them, I know not.

I ask of him, "Is it not so that all the words of the Terrible One were but lies and blasphemy and sacrilege?"

He replies:

"Thou hast entered into the hall of the Empty One, and hast met him face to face. Thou didst overcome by Silence. Now dost thou wish to slay the Devil with his own weapons? Be content."

He turns and departs.

Suddenly, I am no longer behind the table, but am standing atop a tall pillar within the silent city which I beheld at the outset of the Vision. Before, I went in wearing a black robe and Crown with crimson cap of maintenance.[21] Now I am wearing a pure white robe with no hood.[22] With arms outstretched I return. Behind me I now hear a choir of Angels singing. All about me I hear the ringing of chimes and bells. I look behind me as the Gate closes.

The Guardian unsheathes his sword, and with it he carves three figures in the door:

[23]

The Vision fades. It is finished.

January 31, 1977 E.V.
10:00 P.M. – 10:45 P.M.

---

[21] Pictured in the frontispiece.
[22] The Robe of the Adeptus Minor (without).
[23] The word 工刀工 is Enochian, IAD, meaning "God."

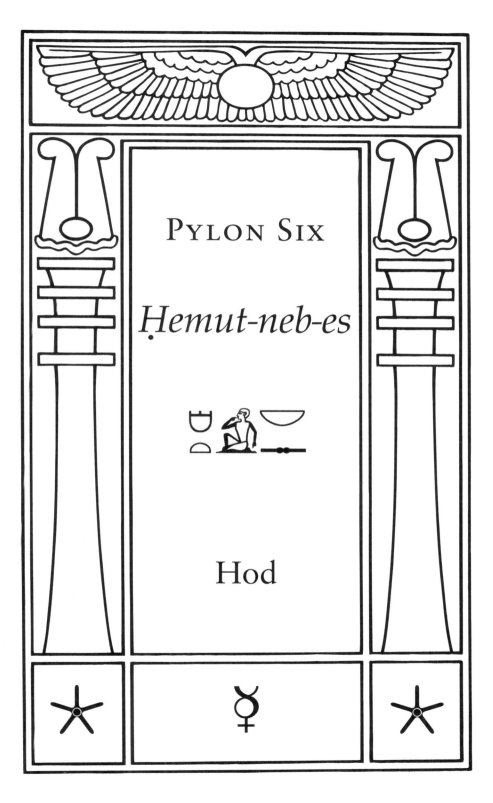

Castor and Pollux (engraving of the Ildefonso Group, Museum of Madrid. Date unknown.)

I AM FALLING DOWN the length of a corridor that is the coils of the twin serpents. It grows smaller and tightens. It is as if I would be crushed in the coils of the serpents. Now, I know this is the restriction of the mind. Tighter and tighter it winds about us until there is no movement. There is no *going* in Mind. The writhing of this serpent is not fulfilling; it only receives and molds and builds itself scale by scale until the body of it grows vast. Thus it is said, thou must slay the serpent.¹

Now I see a looming figure of Tahuti, so large I cannot comprehend it. Both hands are held out, and in his hands stand two naked children. They are dancing as if in a ballet. They are Castor and Pollux.² (It is so difficult to talk!)

At the heart of Tahuti I see the symbol of ☿. Now I have come to know that this is the lower palace of *He Who Utters*³ whereby the worlds are loosed to tread the path of *māyā*.⁴ And I speak unto the figure, "Take me to the Angel of the Pylon, so that I pierce the mysteries and take unto my breast the knowledge of the Sanctuary."

Immediately the image of Tahuti and that of the twins vanish.

---

¹ The phrase "slay the serpent" probably refers to the Hindu legend wherein Krishna commands Arjuna to kill the snake Ashvasena, saying "slay the serpent, for he has become your enemy." (*Mahābhārata*, Book 8, *Karna Parva*, Chapter 4.)

² Castor and Pollux are Latin names for Κάστωρ and Πολυδεύκης, the twins who were collectively known as the Διόσκουροι, "sons of Zeus." In Latin they are known as *Gemini*. In the Vision they signify the zodiacal sign of ♊ which is ruled by ☿.

³ "He Who Utters" is the Magus. Chokmah is reflected into this Pylon by reason of Mercury.

⁴ माया "illusion" (Sanskrit), considered the manifestation of illusion and duality in the phenomenal world.

I see an Angel approaching bearing a sword encrusted with jewels. He holds the blade upright to divide the Crown.

And I address him saying, "ELOHIM TzABAOTH ARARITA."[5]

Suddenly, he takes the sword and slashes across my breast, making a great gash. But there is no blood and there is no pain. He says:

"This is Satan divided against Satan. How shall his kingdom stand? Verily, it shall not stand but fall in that day."[6]

And I say unto him, "Take me unto the Pylon. Grant unto me the mystery."

He replies:

"It is well."

---

[5] אלהים צבאות אראריתא *Elohim Tzabaoth* is the God-name attributed to Hod in Assiah. When performing the Invoking Hexagram of ☿ the word *Ararita* is appended. Ararita is a Notariqon for the phrase, אחד ראש אחדותו ראש יחוד תמורתו אחד. "One is His beginning; One is His individuality; His Permutation One." (From the *Sepher Ha-Iyyun (Book of Contemplation)*. See Adolf Jelinek, *Auswahl kabbalistischer Mystik: Heft I. Zum Theil nach Handschriften zu Paris und Hamburg, nebst historischen Untersuchungen und Charakteristiken*, page 10.)

[6] Cf. Matthew 12:25–26, "And Jesus knew their thoughts, and said unto them, 'Every kingdom divided against itself is brought to desolation; and every city or house divided against itself shall not stand. And if Satan cast out Satan, he is divided against himself; how shall then his kingdom stand?'" (AV). The Sword is the weapon of the intellect, and we are our own worst enemy. The intellect cannot be used to achieve Unity, but merely endless division of itself by analysis. Cf. Crowley, *Book IV*, Part II, Chapter VIII, The Sword: "As we are below the Abyss, this weapon is entirely destructive: it divides Satan against Satan." The action of the angel in the vision was not accompanied with any pain or discomfort. It was purely symbolic.

He turns and makes his way down an avenue of sphinxes. They are curious sphinxes, wearing hostile expressions as it were. It is if they are full of the wrath of God and lie in wait to spring upon the unwary. Now I see the Pylon ahead. In the midst of the path there is a large fountain of clear water. It is like the Two of Cups with twin fishes entwined, yet there is only one cup to receive the water. It is flanked by a white and a black pillar. Across the top of the Pylon there is an ancient writing carved in the stone. It is so old that I cannot make out the words.

The Angel speaks and says:

"It is no worry, for they are but lies. Pass thou on."[7]

And now I enter the gates, and behold! A beautiful city with hanging gardens and statues of many gods.[8]

From some unseen point a voice cries out:

"O how beautiful thou art in all thy ways! Thy majesty defieth my tongue! I am rapt away in the fullness of thy kisses, o city of the Ibis![9] Yet it repenteth me that I have made thee!"

He weeps and moans and his cries echo throughout the city. And I say unto the Angel, "Why does he weep so? Is the city not grand and full of majesty?"

---

[7] All of these landmarks, the sphinxes and the fountain, were aspects of my mind. Likewise the writing upon the Pylon, which the Angel reminds me are mere constructions of the Ruach and not Truth.

[8] The city signified my Intellect (the Ruach, or Hexad of the Reasoning Faculty, comprising the Sephiroth Chesed through Yesod). Cf. *Liber LXV*, III:21, where the mind of Frater Perdurabo is described as "the great city, the city of the violets and the roses."

[9] "Ibis," derived from Egyptian 𓉔𓃀𓅞 *hby* (Coptic ϩⲓⲃⲱⲓ), is referred to Tahuti, hence ☿. The "City of the Ibis" is the Mind.

He replies:

"Verily, and herein is the twofold nature of the serpent. He is wise, yet he bears a poison within the hollow of his jaws and he doth infect the body with pleasure. He doth rear himself up and declare, 'I am the first and I am the last. I shall die not, who hath created all.' And though his spittle is venom and from his mouth run seas of poison, he is exalted to the pinnacles of the earth and truth abideth not."[10]

I say unto the Angel, "This do I perceive. Thus was it written, 'Seek the equation.'"[11]

The Angel replies:

"It cannot be spoken."

I turn again unto the Guardian and say, "I ask that I might learn of a certain secret, yet I fear to name it."[12]

---

[10] The intellect can be a lovely construction, yet despite its beauty, it is below the Abyss, and inherently flawed. The ego declares itself to be the Crown of incarnation, the Alpha and Omega, the First and the Last, the creator of all things. Despite this falsehood, the intellect is idolized and idealized. Truth (that which contains its own opposite) is above Reason altogether.

[11] See the Fifth Pylon.

[12] I wanted to learn the secret of *Liber MCXXXIX*, "The Utterance of the Pythoness," attributed to ☿. The Liber is not extant but is listed in *Liber Viarvm Viæ*. The number 1139 assigned to the Liber is the value of δελφύς, "womb." The word δελφύς is derived from the same root as Δελφοι, "Delphi," the site where Apollo slew the Python who lived there and guarded the navel (ὀμφᾰλός) of the earth. This was also the site of the Oracle of Delphi, the Priestess called the πυθία, Pythia (from πύθων, Python). The Priestess delivered her Oracles while seated upon a tripod, hence the Tripod in *Liber 777* is attributed to ☿. Crowley's note

The Angel answered:

"Thy desire is already known, and thus it shall be so. But thou must first prepare thyself for the revelation. Return unto thy place until the appointed hour. Prepare a certain Pantacle of ☽ in the colors of the Queen.[13] Prepare thy disciple to be scribe to thy word, for it is not permitted that he who sees shall write. And he must bind himself by Oath that he not reveal the way of this great mystery. After thou dost behold, shalt thou destroy the writing, for none may partake save they partake face to face with the dreadful one.[14] Depart now, and return at the appointed hour, and ye shall commune with the Mighty Oracle."

I do as I am commanded, and return to the body. The Aire is shut up until the time that hath been revealed unto me.

January 14, 1977 E.V.
7:10 P.M. – 8:10 P.M.

---

to the attribution reads, "The Tripod would appear at first sight to be Lunar; but this is wrong. The real connection is with ATU VI, the 'Oracle of the Mighty Gods' (*777 and Other Qabalistic Writings of Aleister Crowley*, p. 111). The Sixth Pylon, part II, among other things, reveals the *modus operandi* for the *Rite of H* as well as the *Rite of ALIM*, being two methods for obtaining the Utterance of the Pythoness.

[13] This was a Pantacle inscribed with the Sigil of Zooωasar from *Liber CCXXXI*. It was constructed of wax and painted in the Queen scale as instructed. Acrylic paint with no water was used because the Pantacle was made of wax.

[14] The original manuscript of the Vision was to be destroyed. It was.

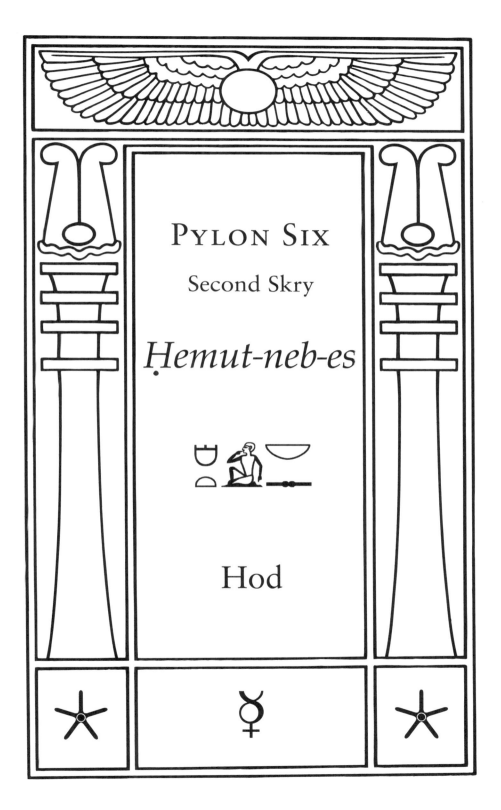

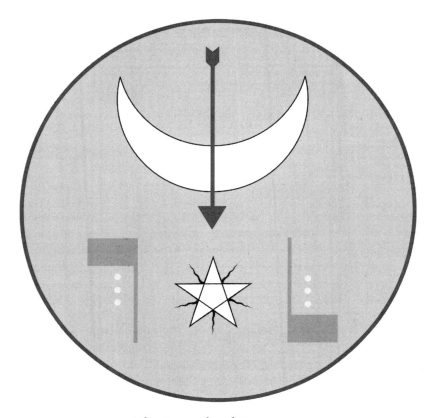

The Pantacle of Zoowasar.
(See insert following page 144.)

THE OATH BY THE SCRIBE

I, Frater I.A.T.A., a Neophyte 1°=10□ of the A∴A∴, do hereby swear upon my honor as a man and a Brother of the G∴D∴, and in full humility before the Lord of the Æon Heru-ra-ha, that I will never divulge that which I have witnessed[1] or scribed pertaining to the mystery of the Sixth Pylon. And I swear that I will not swerve in my duties nor falter in my task, as long as there is life left in me.

Witness mine hand
I. A. T. A.
1°=10□ A∴A∴

NOTE: I was instructed to wear a Yellow Cape over my black Robe with the emblem of the Rosy Cross upon the breast; the Scribe was to wear an Orange Cape over the Robe of a Probationer. I was to Open the Temple by wielding the Wand and Banishing with the Pentagram of Air and with the Hexagram of Mercury, followed by the Invoking Pentagram of Air and the Invoking Hexagram of Mercury. The Scribe, who was instructed to bear the Sword, was then to trace the symbols ⎤ and ⌊ respectively toward Boleskine. He was then to seat himself in front of me and prepare to write what I dictated. I then took the Pantacle, which was wrapped in Yellow Silk, from the altar, and removed the Silk. I seated myself behind the Scribe in the Dragon *āsana* with the Pantacle on the floor before me. Formulating the image of the Pantacle astrally before me, I assumed the god-form as prescribed and passed through it to the Pylon before me.

---

[1] At times, the Scribe was able to see what I was observing in the vision.

$\mathcal{T}$HERE IS A CLEFT IN THE SKY and the Voice is thundering out:

"ODO QO KI KIKALE![2]
  I do lift up my sword and split the vulva of He-She the queen! I am of the black dog!"[3]

There is a bright light of vivid orange. I can see no face in the center, though it is the source of the Voice. The light has no sound in itself. A spot of darkness now appears in the midst of the bright light. It is impossible to describe this. It is like a hole in space. A hole.

The Voice speaks again:

"I stand in the midst and who shall know who is Asi and who is Nephthi?[4]
  I am Upright and I am Averse.[5]
  I am the Upper Axe and I am the Lower Axe.[6]
  I am the God and I am the Dog. It is impure that thou shouldst spy upon this in all its wholeness, for though the dead are led by the dogs, of the *certain* Dead, only the Black Ones may know."[7]

---

[2] Enochian, ⌁⌁ ⌁ ⌁ ⌁⌁⌁. "Open or conceal the mysteries!"

[3] The Black Dog refers to Hermanubis. The Greeks merged the figure of Anubis with Hermes and called him Hermanubis. The city of his cult was Cynopolis, which means "city of dogs." He, like Anubis, was the guide of the dead.

[4] Asi = Isis or Nature. Nephthi = Nephthys or Perfection. Cf. *Liber CCXXXI*, 6: "Here then beneath the winged Eros is youth, delighting in the one and the other. He is Asar between Asi and Nephthi; he cometh forth from the veil." This verse corresponds to ℸ and the Sigil of Zoowasar.

[5] IAO/OAI.

[6] The "axes" refer to the dual signs on the Sigil that resemble the Egyptian hieroglyph of Neter ⌁, which signifies divinity.

[7] The "*certain* Dead" indicates The Masters of the Temple in Binah, the

Now I see the black hole split apart and become a great gash. It is a vast rip in the sky.[8]

Suddenly I see a large naked woman and between her legs there is a monstrous serpent crawling out like molten lava.[9]

He winds himself about her legs, first one, then the other, and lastly her body. He flicks his tongue in her face and she is in ecstasy. Her passion mounts until she is lost in the throes of lust. He bites her over the length of her body, sinking his fangs into the folds of her soft flesh. Yet, it is not causing her pain.

Her ecstasy only grows until she cries out:

"I will suck up the poison my Lord!"

It is like a dance in slow motion. She tries to speak again but the words will not come.

The Serpent speaks:

"I have fathered the bastards of the blackened Earth. I have traced my tongue along the silken thighs of the naked one."

Suddenly, she screams:

"I am with Child!"

Immediately, I see behind them two vast faces, enormous heads seemingly the same.

Another Voice cries out:

"Behold! This is a Mystery, corrupted and defiled by the

"Black Ones" who absorb all, and reflect naught. The Color of Binah is black in the Queen Scale.

[8] Cf. *Liber A'Ash*, 3.

[9] Lilith, the serpent-woman. Cf. *Liber LXV*, III:3–12.

ancient Qabalists. As it is written, 'There is the upward Arrow and there is the downward Arrow. There is the Arrow from the Sun into the mouth of the dead Father.'[10] Thus, it was concealed in the script of Khem[11] whereby Hoor did give sustenance to his father Asar, and did give to him for meat the Eye. And further, 'My buttocks are the buttocks of the Eye of Hoor.'"[12]

He speaks of the legend of Adam and Eve:

"Thus it was spoken corruptly of the legend of Eve and the Serpent, she who is Lilith. For Cain was indeed the child of the Serpent. But in this mystery, Eve and Adam are one. Thus, in Coptic, the name of Cain is 81."[13]

Something is being said about Hanuman the monkey god and Anubis.
I see an image of a monkey astride the back of Lilith.[14]
This is all disconnected idea. There are no words. I see a fleeting image of the dual god Heru-em-Anpu whose name means "Dog in the Sun."[15]

---

[10] זרע. This arrow is from the bow of Eros (ז) inspired by Apollo (ר). The mouth of the dead father is the Eye of Hoor (ע).

[11] I.e. Egypt.

[12] From *The Egyptian Book of the Dead*, Spell 42, the "Proclamation of the Perfected One." Compare *Initiation in the Æon of the Child*, Appendix I.

[13] Cain in Coptic = ⲔⲀⲒⲚ = 20 + 1 + 10 + 50 = 81. This refers to the Magical formula of ALIM, for which see *Book IV*, Part 3, Chapter IV. It is also worth noting that in Hebrew, Cain = קין = 160 = צלם "image."

[14] Cf. *Liber Ararita*, II:10. See also *Liber 418*, 3rd Æthyr.

[15] 𓅃𓅓𓃣 ḥr-m-inpw, literally "Horus with Anubis." The Greeks confounded the words ḥr-m with Hermes and called him Hermanubis, who is depicted with the head of a dog. Horus, ḥr, is solar, hence the

Lilith — by John Collier (1892).

Hermanubis
From Vollmer, *Wörterbuch der Mythologie aller Völker* (1874).

The Voice begins to speak of the Hebrew legend again:

"When Cain had murdered his brother he was cast out and the earth was made barren. Cursed is the ground which hath opened its PEH to receive thy brother's blood from thine own YOD.[16]

And he dwelt in the land of Nod, which is another way of writing *The Arrow*.[17]

And he knew his wife and begat Enoch.[18]

For Enoch was the Father of the Voice among the Jews. Thus are my Children the Children of the Voice.

FOR I AM THE ORACLE OF THE MIGHTY GODS![19]

My Children are Romulus and Remus, nursed by the Wolf, who didst set the City upon the Seven Hills.[20] In the Outer World, shalt thou use this Secret to scale the Seven Hills. For in the Outer, it goeth no further.

Upon the first hill shall stand the Kings and Rulers.

Sun, and Anubis, *inpw* the "dog" in the sun. The inference is that Hoor = God, Anubis = Dog, upright and averse, mirror images of one another. There is yet another interpretation which is referred to the formula of ALIM.

[16] Genesis 4:11, "And now art thou cursed from the earth, what hath opened her mouth to receive thy brother's blood from thy hand." (AV)

[17] Genesis 4:16, "And Cain went out from the presence of the Lord, and dwelt in the land of Nod, on the east of Eden." (AV) Nod = נוד = 60 = ס, Atu XIV = ♐.

[18] Genesis 4:17, "And Cain knew his wife; and she conceived, and bare Enoch." (AV)

[19] The Mystical name of Atu VI, "The Lovers" (or Brothers).

[20] Romulus and Remus, half-divine twins, suckled by a she-wolf, and the founders of the city of Rome, called the "City of the Seven Hills." In the Vision, the Seven Hills signify the seven lower Sephiroth. The names of the seven hills of Rome are worth noting: Aventine, Caelian, Capitoline, Esquiline, Palatine, Quirinal and Viminal.

Atu VI: The Lovers — Thoth Tarot

Upon the second, Warriors of mighty Strength who shed blood for the cause of freedom.

Upon the third hill may the Gold be forged in a furnace of desire. Yet, few are they who have sought the Holy One through this portal.

Upon the fourth hill stand Lovers in full attire, brought to thee for thy pleasure.

On the fifth hill, Wisdom and Knowledge stand in an open book, written by the stylus of the divine.

On the sixth hill rest the beds of the Diviners; those who speak with Tongues and those who partake of strange drugs and Sanctify by means of their wine-bibbing.

On the last hill shalt thou find the Riches and Avenues to the Kingdom.[21]

Yet, despite their Glory and Power, seek not these lest ye fall away from the manifestation of the Voice. Rather, let there be two well-prepared in the ways of the Art. And one shall be the King to administer the Poison sucked up by the Children of the Voice. And the second, He-She the Queen, to suffer the charms of the Snake. And in the moment of rejoicing shall the Venom corrode the interior parts of the Earth.[22] Her mouth shall be split and she will roar in rapture as the Dæmon pervadeth the Soul.

This is of the way to be ordained.[23]

Yet, those who would come to know the way of the Seven Hills may lap up the Spittle of the Dragon.[24] Yet, let

---

[21] The seven hills in order are: ♃, ♂, ☉, ♀, ☿, ☽ and ♄.

[22] *Visita Interiora Terrae Rectificando Invenies Occultum Lapidem.* V.I.T.R.I.O.L. Cf. *Liber CCXX*, II:26.

[23] The meaning of this is obscure.

[24] Dragon, תנינם = 550 = 55 × 10 or Σ(1–10), the mystic number of Malkuth = מלכית = 496 = Σ(1–31) where 31 = אל (God) and לא (Not). The word "dragon" is derived from δράκων, literally "seeing one" (𓂀). In *The Zohar*, it is said that the Dragon "raiseth his head at the back of

their breath stink with the stink of Roses. And who shall know what is the head and what is the Tail of Leviathan?[25] Let the Goddess shriek, for with the Fishhook let them draw out Mazzaroth in his season.[26]

In the end, let all return to the hollow of the Great Sea.[27]

Of that which lies beyond, No Man[28] may know."

The Voice has ceased, and the tear in the sky has closed itself. Once again, I see the black hole in the midst of the orange rays.

Now, I see the appearance of two images on the left and right, of which I may not speak lest I divulge a secret of the Vision.[29]

All is quiet. It is over.

January 15, 1977 e.v.
12:00 midnight – 12:50 a.m.

---

the bride of Microprosopus, where is the place of the most severe judgments."(Mathers, *The Kabbalah Unveiled*, pp. 51–52.)

[25] The head = Caput Draconis ☊, the tail = Cauda Draconis ☋. Leviathan = לויתן = 496 = מלכית = ☿.

[26] An obscure reference. In the book of Job, 38:32, Yahweh questions Job, "Canst thou bring forth Mazzaroth in his season?" Mazzaroth is from Greek μαζουρωθ which is from the Hebrew plural מזרית which is a *hapax legomenon* in the Bible. It is possibly a form of מסלות, "zodiac." The generally accepted meaning is simply the Signs of the Zodiac, although it remains uncertain. If Mazzaroth refers to the Zodiac, drawing him out with Tzaddi the fishhook may refer to the letter ה and "The Star" in some way.

[27] Binah. Note that the word Zayin spelled in full = זין = 67 = בינה.

[28] Nemo, the Magister Templi. The highest forms of these mysteries are beyond the Abyss.

[29] Cf. *Liber LXVI*, 8.

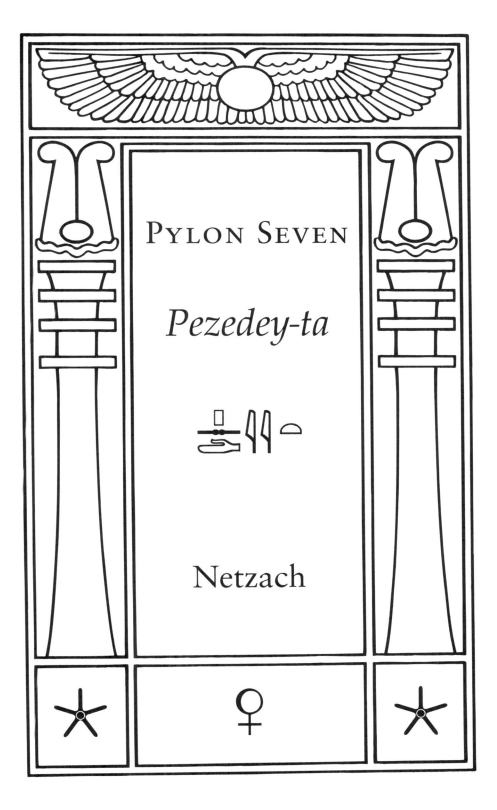

$\mathcal{M}$Y ENTIRE VISION is of a swirling emerald green sea. It gives the appearance of a whirlpool, except that its motion changes—first deosil, then widdershins.

Also, there is a faint mist hovering above the surface of the water, and I am aware that this is the brooding Spirit ELOHIM.[1]

Now there is a Voice:

"Come thou who will and enter my Gates, Daughter of the Mighty Ones,[2] Queen of the lustral waters which are the pools of happiness."

Immediately the Vision changes and becomes a gleaming, pure white. I can see the Pylon now, but it is completely beyond description. It is absolutely blinding and it gleams so that I cannot make out the shape of it.

Before the entrance, I now see three guardians. The one on the left is holding a Cube. The one in the center is holding Scales. And the one on the right is holding a Cube that has been folded out to form a Cross.[3]

I give them the Sign of the Philosophus so that I may pass. Receiving the Sign, they merely smile and stand aside.[4] I pass through the passageway and begin to walk down a street built of cobblestones. All around me everything is blinding to the sight.

---

[1] The Ruach Elohim, רוח אלהים, "Spirit of God," the "Holy Spirit." See Genesis 1:1–2.

[2] "Daughter of the Mighty Ones" is the Mystical Title of Atu III, "The Empress" (♀).

[3] The cube = ד, the Scales = ל, the Cube folded out to form a Cross = ת. Thus דלת = ♀.

[4] I was not yet fully a Philosophus. There was something quite patronizing in their smiles, for they recognized my spiritual immaturity.

Now before me I see a Goddess hovering in mid-air.
She bears something in her left hand but I cannot make it out.
Now I see it. It is a sistrum.[5]
I speak to her, "Art thou the Guardian of this sphere?"[6]

---

[5] The sacred instrument of Hathor ☥.

[6] Here, and in several other places in these Visions, I used the term "sphere," which is incorrect. "Sephira" does not mean "sphere," nor are the Sephiroth bound to any such geometrical concept. "Sephira" means "number" or "emanation." While graphically represented as a circle in two dimensional diagrams, or a sphere in three dimensional models, this is merely a convenience of expression.

She replies:

"Nay. O thou who hath turned a deafened ear! I would press thee to my breast, but thou wouldst not! I would crush thee in rapture and drink the dregs of delight, but thou wouldst not! I would smother thee with kisses in the House of the Hawk, but thou wouldst not! I would lay blossoms in the path that thou dost tread, to soothe the soles of thy feet, but thou wouldst not!"

I am stunned by the beauty of her presence and I cry out, "I pray thee, grant me the perfume of thy nostrils so that I may cool my skin!"
She says:

"I would grant thee the Breath of Life that molds Clay into God[7] if thou wouldst but hear the echo of my faint murmurings in the Halls of Love."

I call out again, "I pray thee to grant me, if but for a moment, the presence of thy majesty! And I beseech thee, who art thou?"
She answers me:

"I am LOVE and I am PERFECTION and I am MATERIAL GAIN. But this is of the CRAB and the RAM and the VIRGIN.[8] But lo! Shalt thou beware me, for I am the ILLUSION OF SUCCESS and this is of the SCORPION![9] And is the Scorpion not Death? And Death is the First Letter of my

---

[7] This "Breath of Life" is the רוח אלהים (Ruach Elohim) which changed the lifeless Clay into Adam, the first man. There is no god but man.

[8] "Love" = "Two of Cups" = ♀ in ♋ (the Crab.) "Perfection" = "Four of Wands" = ♀ in ♈ (the Ram.) "Material Gain" = "Nine of Pentacles" = ♀ in ♍ (the Virgin).

[9] "Illusion of Success" = "Seven of Cups" = ♀ in ♏ (the Scorpion).

Name, who doth set the Emperor upon my Holy Word 418.[10] Is not the Gate the Balance of the Universe?"[11]

And I say, "Press me to thy breast! And press thy lips to mine, if but for a moment!"

She begins to speak in another tongue. It is Egyptian and she said:

"There is the dove, and there is the serpent."[12]

Somehow, I understand her speech and I answer her and say, "This is the place of the dove."

From her robe, she now withdraws a scroll with Egyptian writing. She unfolds it for me to read. It says:

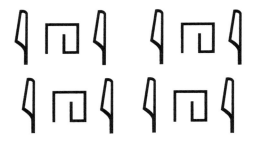

Immediately, the tenor of the Vision changes. Behind her I see a most beautiful sunset and the cry of AHA is being repeated by Voices from some unseen place.[13] It sounds as if hundreds

---

[10] "Death" (נ) + "The Emperor" (צ) + My Holy Word 418 (ח in full = חית = 418). Thus, נצח, Netzach.

[11] The Gate (ד) the Balance (ל) of the Universe (ת). Thus דלת = Daleth = ♀.

[12] *Liber CCXX*, I:57.

[13] The revelation of these words came as a surprise to me. I knew the magical word AHA, and would have expected to see the hieroglyphics

of Angels are chanting the cry. It is very loud and I can hear it resounding throughout the Aire.

Now the Goddess has disappeared. I can see something approaching. It is a Wheel, spinning rapidly in a clockwise direction.[14] It comes to stand before me, still spinning.

Now a Voice calls out from the center of the Wheel:

"Thou hast sought the Twenty and Eight Powers. Behold the Mystic Wheel 418.
"KAPH – PEH – ChETH!"[15]

From out of the Wheel a Dove wings its way into the Heavens bearing olive branches. It ascends into the sky and disappears. As I cast my eyes back to the Wheel, I see a large Archway behind it. And I ask, "What standeth yonder?"

A Voice answers me:

"Behold the Gate to the Pastos! Thou mayest not yet pass this way, for thy day hath not come when thou shalt be One Hundred and Twenty."[16]

---

written 𓃒 3h3, or AHA, meaning "Cow," an animal sacred to Hathor. Afterwards, I discovered that the word as written in the Vision, transliterated as *ihi*, means "a cry of joy."

[14] This is a very important detail. In the old Marseilles style Tarot decks, the wheel is turning *counterclockwise*. But in the *Thoth Tarot* of Thelema, the opposite is shown. "The Wheel" of the Thelemic Tarot is turning *clockwise*.

[15] The traditional Password of the Philosophus was כח which means "power." The phrase "Mystic wheel 418" is a cipher. פ + כ is Kaph spelled in full כף = Atu X, "The Wheel," and 418 = ח spelled in full חית.

[16] The mystical age of our Father and Brother C.R.C. Also the number of עו, ON, City of the Sun. This all refers to the Grade of Adeptus Minor.

Atu X: Fortune (The Wheel) — Thoth Tarot

I speak again, being filled with yearning, "I long to pass on!" The Voice replies:

"And so thou shalt, when the Work is accomplished. For thou dost stand upon the Portal."

I continue, "I pray thee for a Vision of that which lieth beyond! For another kiss from the Holy One!"[17]

And it is granted unto me. Even as the Bride awaits the Bridegroom, I wait to catch a glimpse of the Bridal Chamber.[18] Although I am afforded a fleeting glimpse of the Sanctuary, I am pushed back into the former Vision. And of that which mine eyes did behold I cannot speak, for my mouth hath closed upon itself like two lovers in the night. I force myself to return to the Vision.

Before me, I now see a large golden statue of Hathor. She has the Sun Disc between her horns and there is a certain secret flame that is playing upon her brow. All I can think of is that which is written in *The Book of the Heart Girt with the Serpent*, "from the low sweet brows of Hathor..."[19]

Suddenly, from either side of the statue, a procession of priests advances. The leader of each column bears fumigations and the air is filled with its fragrance. It is a beautiful scent and I think of Jasmine, Rose and Hyacinth.[20] The second priest in each column lays down rose petals before the Goddess.

Now all the priests kneel before the altar and begin to sing:

> "House of the Hawk,
>   Shrine of the Falcon,

---

[17] The Holy Guardian Angel.

[18] The Bridal Chamber is Tiphereth.

[19] *Liber LXV*, II:34.

[20] Jasmine suggests the sensuality of Venus as the Sacred Harlot, the Rose her Love, and the Hyacinth represents her as the Virgin of Eternity.

>   Mother to whom"
>   Power is given,
>   Mistress of mirth
>   and sweet caresses."[21]

From behind the Shrine, there is a refrain:

"VAHYEH, VAHYEH, VAHYEH, VAHYEH."[22]

Now the crown of the Goddess' head has opened and a tremendous flame has gone out reaching into the Heavens. I cannot see the end of it! It reaches into Eternity! Words cannot begin to describe this! The flame is silent and licking in appearance.

It looks as if it would be cold as ice!

(Impressions are leaping in my brain!)

I see something very strange. Upon the breast of the statue, I see the number 77. And I am given to know that this is that which is written in *The Book of the Law*, "Choose ye well!"[23]

All the priests are still kneeling silently before the shrine. From the midst of the statue I see transparent images of Hoor-paar-kraat emerge. They come toward me and disappear. (There were three of them.) They were colorless in their transparency and this seems important.

I hear a Voice:

"These are my Children, yet unborn!"

---

[21] All attributes of Hathor.

[22] This is obscure. It appears to be והיה. In the Twelve Banners of the Name יהוה, this form corresponds to the Path of ל which is ruled by ♀. (See *Liber 777*, Column CXL.) Like AHA, it occurs four times, perhaps to indicate Daleth. But the meaning remains unknown.

[23] *Liber CCXX*, I:57 again. 77 is the number of עז, the goat. One should not go to a goat's house for wool.

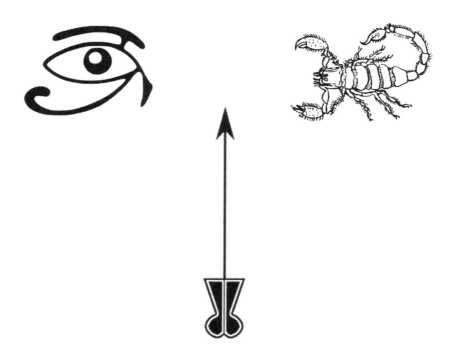

Behind the statue, I now see a vast image of Ra-Hoor-Khuit. The Voice cries:

"These are my Children who lurk unseen!"

Instantly, the Vision is blotted out and there is total blackness. I hear the Voice again:

"And this is their coalition!"[24]

The blackness remains, but I hear a different Voice singing:

---

[24] Cf. the 0 = 2 equation. (+1) + (−1) = 0.

"Gate to ON
City of the Sun!
Bright and Evening Star!"

And I am smothered with thousands of kisses over the entire length of my body. In my brain there burns three images: An EYE, a SCORPION, and in the midst, THE ARROW. [25]

Now I seem to be falling down the shaft of the Arrow. Above me, I can still see the EYE and the SCORPION. I am returned.

February 5, 1977 E.V.
11:30 P.M. – 12:10 A.M.[26]

---

[25] The Eye = ע, the Scorpion = נ, thus עןׂ City of the Sun (Tiphereth). The Arrow is the path of ס. These are the three paths that lead from the Outer College to Tiphereth.

[26] The Skry of the seventh Pylon was hurried and omitted several important procedures of the Invocation. This doubtless explains why the goddess scolded me for my obstinate behavior. The Scribe for this Pylon was Frater O.N.E., a Student who had requested the opportunity, to which I. A.T.A. agreed.

Appendix I

The Names of the Pylons— their Attributions and their Guardians

1: ▽ of ▽ The Name of the Pylon is 𓈉 Zemyeta, *"Western Desert"*
The Guardian is 𓅂𓂝𓈉 Zau Zemyeta *"The Desert"*

2: △ of ▽ The Name of the Pylon is 𓊹𓊹𓊹𓊹𓊹 Sepede-ta-wawau, *"Piercing Flame"*
The Guardian is the Serpent One 𓊹𓅂𓏥𓂋𓆗 Qab-eya, *"Coiled One"*

3: ▽ of ▽ The Name of the Pylon is 𓊹𓊹𓊹 Nebeta-za-tzefu, *"Mistress of Nourishment"*
The Guardian is the Serpent One 𓊹𓏥𓆗 Tzedebeya, *"Stinging One"*

4: △ of ▽ The Name of the Pylon is 𓊹𓏥𓊹 Eiry-ta, *"Doer"*
The Guardian is the Serpent One 𓊹𓆗 Teka-hor, *"Flaming Face"*

5: ☽ The Name of the Pylon is 𓊹𓊹 Nebeta-aḥau, *"Lady of Lifetime"*
The Guardian is the Serpent One 𓊹𓂋𓆗 Seta-ma-eiri-fa, *"Burns with his Eye"*

6: ☿ The Name of the Pylon is 𓊹𓊹𓊹 Ḥemut-neb-es, *"Talisman of its Lord"*[1]

---

[1] This reading is etymologically derived, based on Coptic ϨΟΜΝΤ, "copper, brass" (Crum, 678a), "copper, bronze" (Çerny, 283–284), < 𓊹, *ḥmt* (Faulkner, 169), hence 𓊹𓊹, *ḥmwt* "craftsman" (i.e. a skilled worker in metal.) Cf. WB III, pp. 85–86) Note 𓊹𓊹, *ḥmt-r* "magic spell" where *ḥmt* "crafts" means a magical work (Faulkner, 170). It is certain that some type of metallic piece or coin is intended by 𓊹𓊹 Ḥemut in the Pylon name. The word "talisman" fits this meaning as it is derived from Arabic طلسم *tilsam*, in turn from Greek τελεσμα, "payment," used in Late Greek to mean "initation or mystery," cf. τελεσμός "completion" < Greek τελέειν, "pay (tax), fulfill" < τέλος "fulfillment,

The Guardian is the Serpent One ⟨hieroglyphs⟩ *Yethy-ma-eiri-fa*, "Steals with his Eye"

7: ♀ The Name of the Pylon is ⟨hieroglyphs⟩ *Pezedey-ta*, "Shining One"
The Guardian is the Serpent One ⟨hieroglyphs⟩ *Akha-na-eiri*, "Shut of Eye"

8: ☉ (Paroketh) The Name of the Pylon is ⟨hieroglyphs⟩ *Bekhekh-eya*, "Glowing One"[2]
The Guardian is the Serpent One ⟨hieroglyphs⟩ *Zeta-hor*, "Burning Face"

9: ☉ The Name of the Pylon is ⟨hieroglyphs⟩ *A'ata-shef-shefetu*, "Great of Respect"
The Guardian is the Serpent One ⟨hieroglyphs⟩ *Wepet-ta*, "Top of the Earth"

10: ♂ The Name of the Pylon is ⟨hieroglyphs⟩ *Tzeserey-ta*, "Sanctified One"[3]
The Guardian is the Serpent One ⟨hieroglyphs⟩ *Sethu*, "Burning One"

---

completion." < Sanskrit root तॄ TAR, "to pass over" (from the same root, तर TARA, "a passage, also a spell for banishing evil spirits. (Skeat, *An Etymological Dictionary of the English Language*, p. 622, Richardson and Johnson. *A Dictionary of Persian, Arabic and English*, p. 974a, Monier-Williams, *A Sanskrit English Dictionary*, p. 438.)

[2] As in glowing from a flame.

[3] "Sanctified One" in the sense of someone or something "set apart" or "cloistered" for a sacred purpose. The word ⟨hieroglyph⟩ *dsr* implies this. As an adjective it can mean simply "holy, sacred" (Faulkner 324), the noun ⟨hieroglyph⟩ *dsrw* means "seclusion," while the noun ⟨hieroglyph⟩ *dsrw* is "holy place" (Faulkner 325).

11: ♃ The Name of the Pylon is ▭ *Sheta-besu,* "*Mysterious Initiation*"
The Guardian is the Serpent One ▭ *Yemy-netu-fa,* "*Within his Poison*"

12: ⁂ (Daath) The Name of the Pylon is ▭ *Dezere-ta-bau,* "*Sacred Souls*"[4]
The Guardians are the Serpent Ones ★▭ *Sabeya,* "*Of the Gate,*" and ▭ *Pekhereya,* "*Circumambulator*"

---

[4] It is worth noting that all previous Eleven Pylons state that when once entered, the Gate or Pylon is ▭ *ḫ3i,* "slammed." This Pylon has two doors; once entered, each one is ▭ *ḥtmir,* "sealed" and it is written, ▭ *ḥwt ḥr b3w imyw imnt,* "Then wail the Ba souls who are in the West!" Be warned.

First Pylon
($\triangledown$ of $\triangledown$)

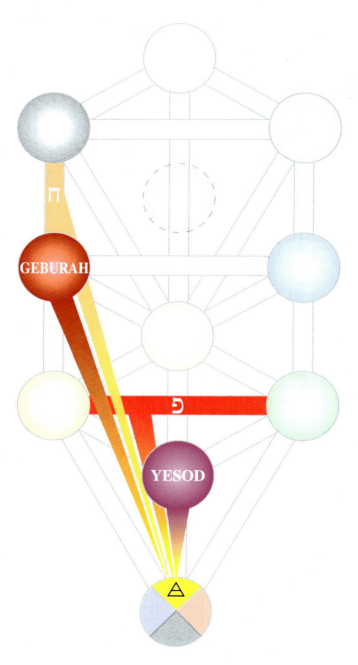

Second Pylon
($\triangle$ of $\triangledown$)

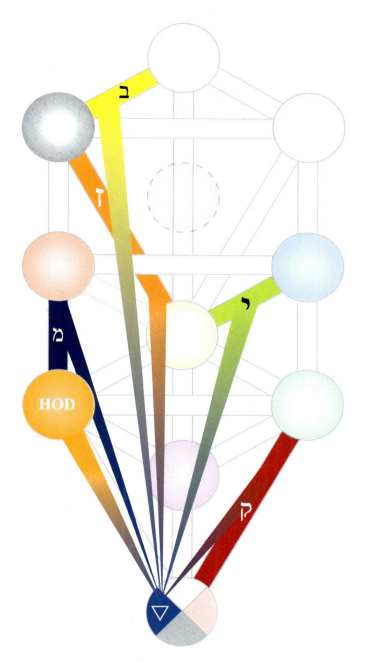

Third Pylon
($\triangledown$ of $\triangledown$)

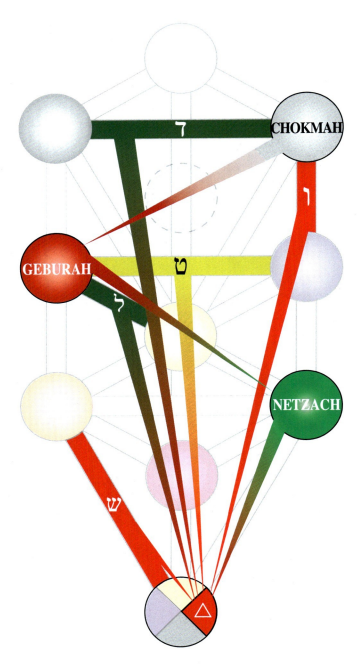

Fourth Pylon
(△ of ▽)

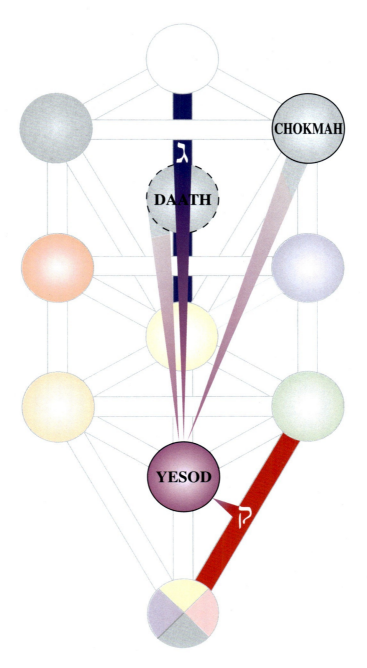

Fifth Pylon
(Yesod)

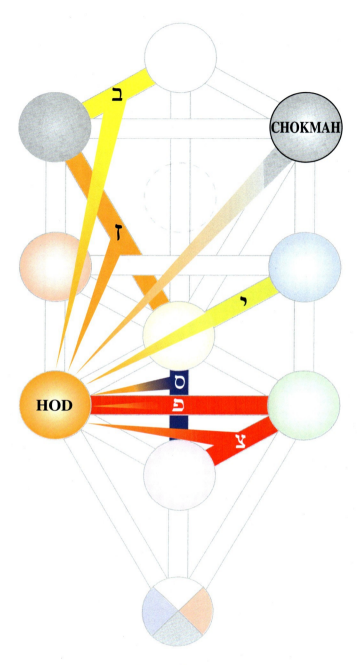

Sixth Pylon
(Hod)

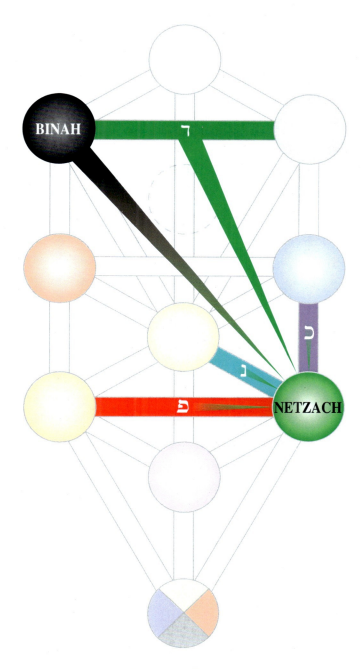

Seventh Pylon
(Netzach)

The Angelic Sigil of Fire

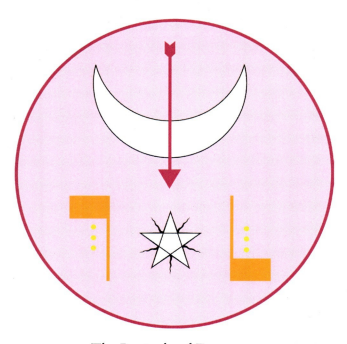

The Pantacle of Zoowasar

Appendix II

The Sigils of the Serpent Ones who are the Guardians of the Pylons

h	*d*	*g*	*b*	*ꜣ*
ẖ	*ḫ*	*ḥ*	*z*	*w*
m	*k*	*y*	*ỉ*	*t*
f	*p*	*ꜥ*	*s*	*n*
ṯ	*š*	*r,l*	*ḳ*	*ḏ*

THE SIGIL GRID is composed of the phonetic sounds for the letters of the ancient Egyptian alphabet. The Grid reads from right to left, top to bottom. The phonetic transliteration of the name of each Guardian serves to form the Sigils.

There is only one square for "r" and "l." Egyptians typically used the hieroglyph of the recumbent lion 🦁 *r*,[1] in late times to spell foreign words with an "l." A good example of this is the name Cleopatra on the Rosetta Stone, which in Egyptian hieroglyphics was spelled 𓎡𓃭𓇋𓅱𓊪𓄿𓂧𓂋𓏏 *krỉwpꜣdrꜣ.t*[2] (i.e. "*qriopadra.t*") to represent the Greek form of the name, ΚΛΕΟΠΑΤΡΑ.[3] Although we transliterate the second character

---

[1] The recumbant lion, Gardiner glyph E23, is a biliteral phonetic value of "*rw*," except when used in group writing, where it represents "*r*" alone. See Gardiner, *Egyptian Grammar*, p. 460. I have personally long believed that this phonetic "r" was "trilled," giving a close approximation to the sound of "l."

[2] The last two hieroglyphics in the name Cleopatra are included to distinguish the name as feminine.

[3] Cf. Champollion, *Lettre à M. Dacier relative à l'alphabet des hiéroglyphes phonétiques*, Paris, 1822.

APPENDIX TWO 147

as "r," it was most likely pronounced as a trilled "r", sounding similar to the Greek Lambda, or phonetic "l." It should be noted that none of the Guardians names include the letter "l."

The Sigil begins with a circle, and ends with a horizontal line. If a letter repeats itself, it is shown on the Sigil as a double loop, as in Guardian #9, *Wepet-ta*. A letter that falls in a direct line with the following letter is indicated by a complete loop before continuing in the straight line, as in Guardian #11, *Yemy-netu-fa*.

※ ※ ※

Below are the Sigils of each of the Guardians, and how they are found on the Sigil Grid.

PYLON ONE
Guardian 1 = Zau Zemyeta = *z3w zmyt*

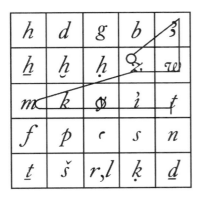
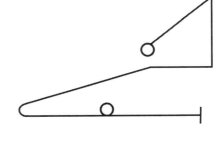

Pylon Two
Guardian = Qab-eya = $ḳ3by$

Pylon Three
Guardian = Tzedebeya = $ḏdby$

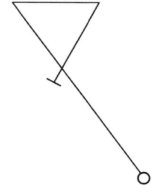

Pylon Four
Guardian = Teka-hor = *tk3-ḥr*

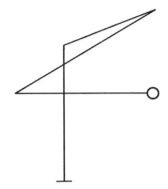

Pylon Five
Guardian = Seta-ma-eiri-fa = *stỉ m ỉrt.f*

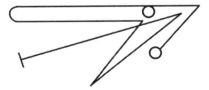

Pylon Six
Guardian = Yethy-ma-eiri-fa = *ity m irt.f*

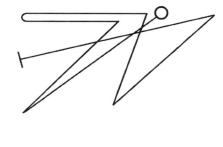

Pylon Seven
Guardian = Akha-na-eiri = *ʿḫn irt*

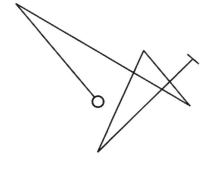

Pylon Eight
Guardian = Zeta-hor = *zty ḥr*

h	*d*	*g*	*b*	*ʒ*
ẖ	*ḫ*	*ḥ*	*z*	*w*
m	*k*	*y*	*ỉ*	*t*
f	*p*	*ꜥ*	*s*	*n*
ṯ	*š*	*r,l*	*q*	*ḏ*

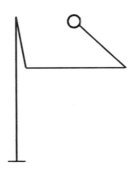

Pylon Nine
Guardian = Wepet-ta = *wp(t)-tʒ*

h	*d*	*g*	*b*	*ʒ*
ẖ	*ḫ*	*ḥ*	*z*	*w*
m	*k*	*y*	*ỉ*	*t*
f	*p*	*ꜥ*	*s*	*n*
ṯ	*š*	*r,l*	*q*	*ḏ*

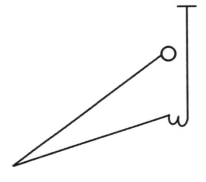

Pylon Ten
Guardian = Sethu = *sṯw*

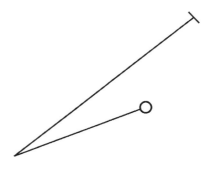

Pylon Eleven
Guardian = Yemy-netu-fa = *imy ntw.f*

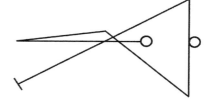

APPENDIX TWO

Pylon Twelve
Guardian 1 = Sabeya = *sb3y*

h	d	g	b	3
ḫ	ẖ	ḥ	z	w
m	k	y	i	t
f	p	ʿ	o	n
ṯ	š	r,l	ḳ	ḏ

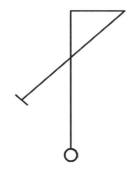

Pylon Twelve
Guardian 2 = Pekhereya = *pẖry*

h	d	g	b	3
ḫ	ẖ	ḥ	z	w
m	k	y	i	t
f	p	ʿ	s	n
ṯ	š	r,l	ḳ	ḏ

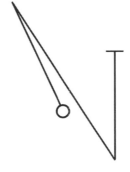

Appendix III

The Images to be Engraved upon the Waxen Seals

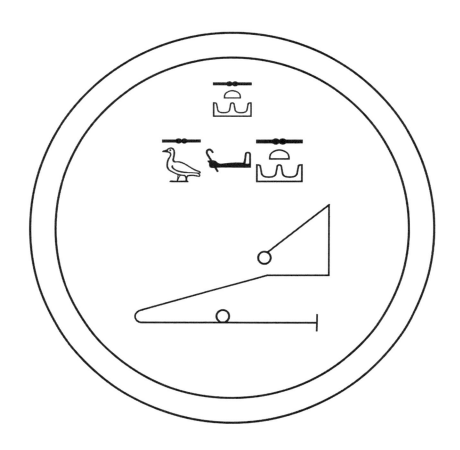

✴ **Pylon One** ✴

Zemyeta

∀ of ∀

Guardian — *Zau Zemyeta*

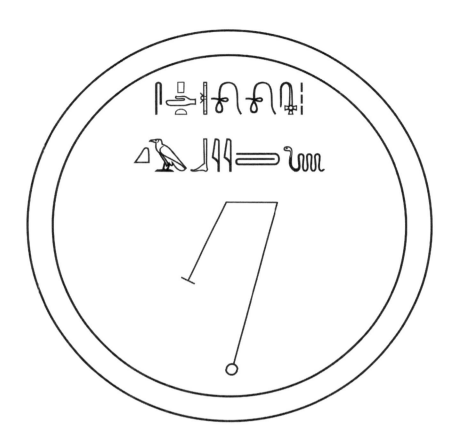

★ Pylon Two ★

Sepedeta-wawau

△ of ▽

Guardian — *Qab-eya*

※ PYLON THREE ※

Nebeta-za-tzefu

▽ of ∀

Guardian — *Tzedebeya*

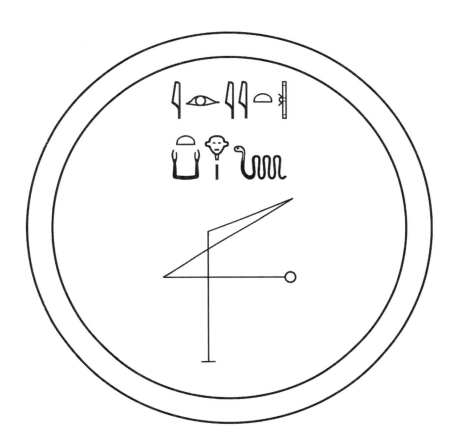

✵ **Pylon Four** ✵

Eiry-ta

△ of ▽

Guardian — *Teka-hor*

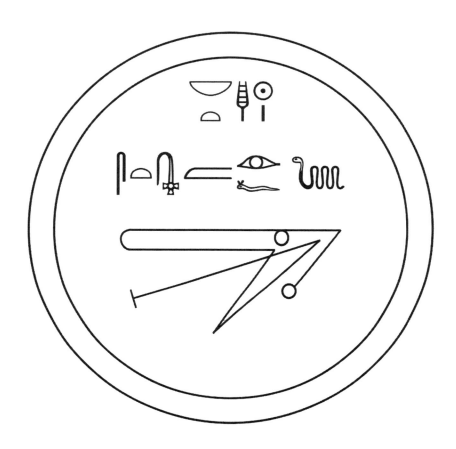

★ Pylon Five ★

Nebeta-aḥau

Guardian — *Seta-ma-eiri-fa*

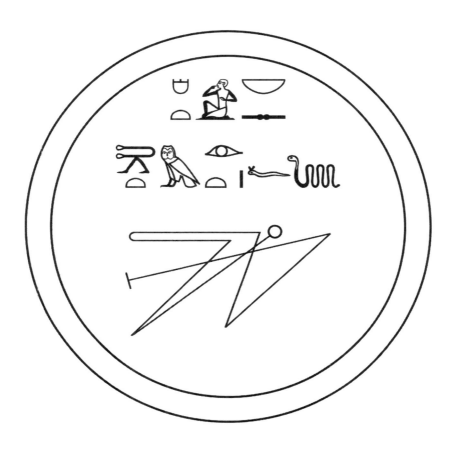

✶ Pylon Six ✶

Ḥemut-neb-es

☿

Guardian — *Yethy-ma-eiri-fa*

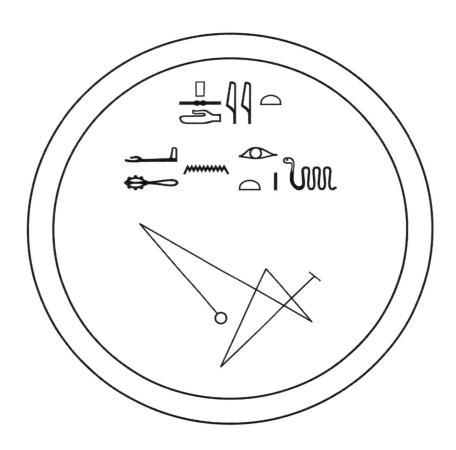

★ Pylon Seven ★

Pezedey-ta

♀

Guardian — *Akha-na-eiri*

Appendix Three

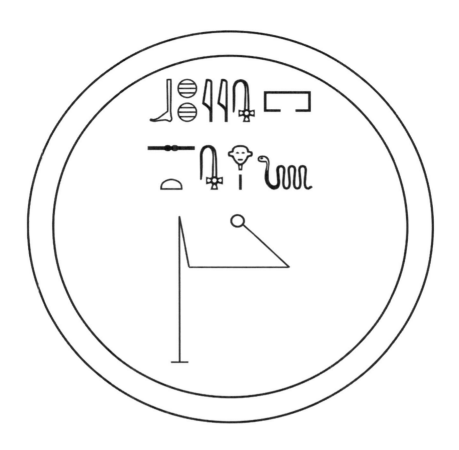

★ Pylon Eight ★

Bekhekh-eya

Guardian — *Zeta-hor*

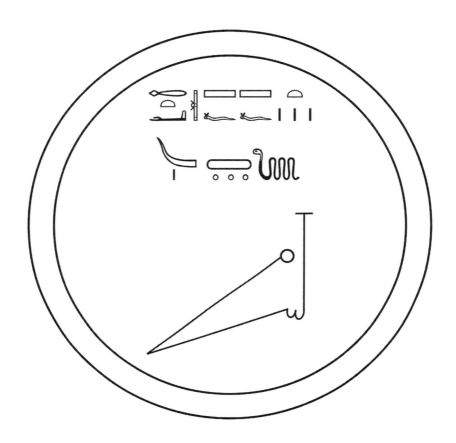

★ Pylon Nine ★

A'ata-shef-shefetu

◉

Guardian — *Wepet-ta*

Appendix Three

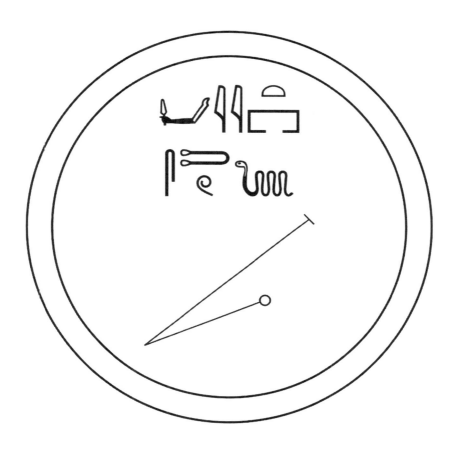

✷ Pylon Ten ✷

Tzeserey-ta

Guardian — *Sethu*

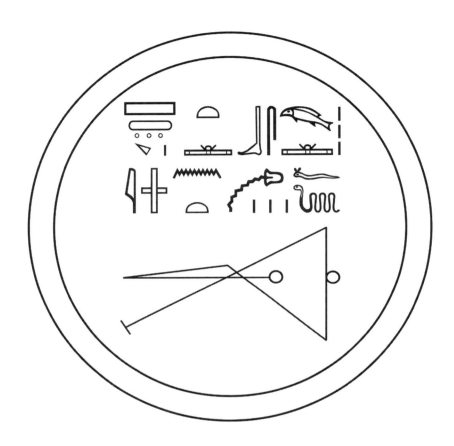

✷ Pylon Eleven ✷

Sheta-besu

♃

Guardian — *Yemy-netu-fa*

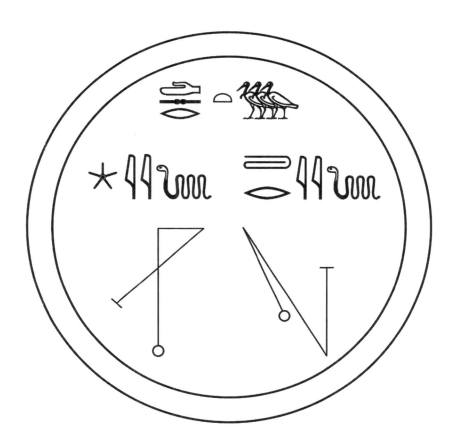

✶ Pylon Twelve ✶

Dezereta-bau

ooo
ooo

Guardians — *Sabeya* and *Pekhereya*

Appendix IV

How to Skry the Pylons

To prepare to skry a Pylon, the Student must first prepare a wax Pantacle with the image of the talismanic figures pertaining to that Pylon, as shown in Appendix III.

Procure a suitable mold for the Pantacle. It should be approximately 6 inches in diameter (15.24 cm), and only ¼ inch in depth (.635 cm). A plastic coffee can lid or margarine lid works quite well. Apply a thin layer of mold release substance, such as vegetable oil, to the inside of the mold. Using plain candle wax or paraffin,[1] using a moderate heat, carefully melt the wax in a metal pot. Carefully pour the hot wax into the mold and let it cool completely.

Remove the wax disk from the mold taking care not to damage it. If the disc has any defects whatsoever, it must be made over.

Referring to the figures in Appendix III above, carefully engrave the wax with a sharp stylus. Wrap the completed Pantacle in black silk and lay it in a cool place until the Ritual.

The Eucharist

Let the aspirant who will be the Seer and the aspirant who will serve as the Scribe prepare the Sacred Cakes of Saffron and Milk & Honey as described in Appendix V.

The Ritual

(1) Let the aspirant who will be the Seer and the aspirant who will serve as the Scribe both bathe immediately prior to the working.

---

[1] In the United States, paraffin is easily obtained in any grocery store that carries supplies for home canning.

(2) Let the Seer and the Scribe both don the Robe of their Grade, but without the Hood.[2]

(3) Upon entering the Temple, let the place be duly prepared. Let the Scribe place the silk-wrapped Pantacle upon the Altar with Lamp, Censer, Bell, Cakes of Saffron, the Cup of Milk and Honey and the paper and pen. The Scribe shall then light the Lamp.

(4) When ready, the Seer shall strike upon the Bell ווווו. Let the Seer Banish the place by the appropriate Signs followed by the appropriate Sign of Invoking. Then let him strike again the Bell וווווו.

(5) Thereupon shall the Scribe kindle the Incense of Abramelin.

(6) The Seer shall then stand, facing the West, while the Scribe stands facing East. Let the Seer make the *Sign of Attack*, and cry aloud:

> *Unity uttermost showed!*
> *I adore the might of thy breath*
> *Supreme and Terrible god,*
> *who makest the gods and death*
> *To tremble before thee!*
> *I, I adore thee!*

Then let the Seer give the *Sign of Defense*.

The Seer and the Scribe shall give the Sign of Adoration singing:

> *A ka dua*
> *tuf ur biu*

---

[2] At the time, I wore a crimson velvet cap of maintenance surmounted by a crown adorned with 3 pentagrams, as in the frontispiece portrait.

APPENDIX FOUR   173

The Sign of Attack (Sign of the Enterer)   *The Sign of Defense (Sign of Silence)*   *The Sign of Adoration*

Bia a'a chefu
Dudu ner af an nuteru!

(7) Let the Seer make the Unicursal Sign of the Crux Ansata and again giving the Sign of Adoration say:

May the gods of the Duant respect me, may they defend their Gates for me, not letting one approach who would do me harm or injure me in the House of Darkness.[3]

(8) Then let both the Seer and Scribe assume the posture of Adoration and let the Scribe cry aloud:

The god Thoth, the king of eternity is with me!
I am Thoth, who made Osiris to be victorious
over his enemies on the day of the weighing of words
in the Great House of Ra, who dwelleth in ON,
City of the Sun!"[4]

---

[3] From *The Egyptian Book of the Dead*, Spell 78, author's translation.
[4] From *The Egyptian Book of the Dead*, Spell 1.

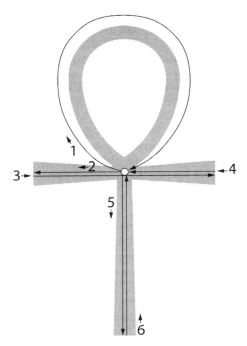

Unicursal Sign of the Crux Ansata.

(9) Let the Seer then proclaim:

Behold! I am Yesterday, Today and Tomorrow!
I am born again and again.
I travel upon high!
I tread upon the firmament of Nu.
I am the Divine Hidden One that created the Gods:
I give offerings to the dwellers in Duant,
the starry abode.[5]

---

[5] Following Crowley's rendition of *The Egyptian Book of the Dead*, Spell 64 variant, with modifications by the author based on the hieroglyphic text.

Appendix Four

(10) The Seer shall then approach the Altar, and strike the Bell ווווו וווווו, take up the Saffron Cakes and the Cup of Milk and Honey, and advance unto the Scribe saying:

Ahathoor hath said, For succor thou shalt take Milk, Honey and Flat Bread that hath no leaven. For corruption shall be without and not within.

(11) He gives the Scribe a Cake of Saffron, and lets him partake of the Milk and Honey. He then places the Cup upon the altar. Then the Scribe shall say,

Thus fortified, I give unto Thee even as I have received.

(12) He gives the Seer a Cake of Saffron, and lets him partake of the Milk and Honey. He returns the Cup to the altar.

(13) The Scribe then takes the silk-wrapped Pantacle, presents it to the Seer, takes up the pen and paper placed upon the Altar.

(14) The Seer shall then assume the chosen *āsana* in his or her station behind the Scribe. The Scribe will then be seated as he or she will, armed with pen and paper, in front of the Seer.

(15) The Scribe shall then assume the god-form of Tahuti. The Seer shall then assume the god-form of Maat.

(16) The Seer shall then unwrap the Pantacle and place it before him on the floor. Then let the Seer cry:

So came I to Duant, the starry abode, and I heard voices crying aloud.

(17) The Seer shall then formulate the image of the Pantacle until it is firm and steady. Let the Seer then pass through this image in the Body of Light clothed in the garment of Maat.

(18) Whatsoever the Seer sees and hears, let it be described as plainly and distinctly as possible and let the Scribe write down that which is heard. Let the Seer speak to any figures he encounters, and insist upon being answered, using the proper pentagram or hexagram as instructed in Appendix VI. Let the Seer be wary lest he or she be deceived by mere appearance or pleasing speech.

(20) When the Vision hath ended, let the Seer and Scribe stand and face the West. The Seer shall say,

> *The light is mine; its rays consume*
>   *Me: I have made a secret door*
> *Into the House of Ra and Tum*
>   *Of Khephra and of Ahathoor.*
> *I am thy Theban, O Mentu*
>   *The prophet Ankh-af-na-khonsu!*
> *By Bes-na-Maut my breast I beat;*
>   *By wise Ta-Nech I weave my spell.*
> *Show thy star-splendour, O Nuit!*
>   *Bid me within thine House to dwell,*
> *O wingèd snake of light, Hadit!*
>   *Abide with me, Ra-Hoor-Khuit!*
> *The ending of the words is the Word Abrahadabra.*

(21) The Seer shall then strike upon the Bell ווווו וווו.

(22) The Seer shall give the Pantacle unto the Scribe who will wrap it once again in the silk cloth. Thereupon, let him break the Pantacle in half within the folds of the cloth.

Let the Seer and Scribe quit the Temple and take the Pantacle to be melted. The wax is then to be poured out, never to be used again.

FINIS

Appendix V

Of the Eucharist, being the Saffron Cakes, Milk and Honey

Saffron Cakes

Ingredients:

1¼	Cup of sifted, white whole wheat Flour (reserve ¼ cup)
1	Teaspoon of Saffron Threads
2 ½	Teaspoons Butter
⅓	Cup Water
½	Teaspoon Kosher Salt

Instructions:

(1) Place Kosher Salt and Saffron Threads in a morter and use the pestle to grind the Saffron and Salt to powder.

(2) Heat the water until it is hot to the touch, but not boiling.

(3) Add the hot water to the Saffron Threads and Salt mixture.

(4) Cover the bowl of Water, Saffron, and Salt. Let it steep for 20 minutes.

(5) Meanwhile, cut the Butter into small chunks.

(6) Add the Butter to 1 cup of Flour and mix gently.

(7) Then add the Saffron-infused Water and stir until mixed.

(8) Dust the work surface with the remaining flour.

(9) Place the dough on the work surface and knead it until it forms a smooth ball.

(10) With a rolling pin, roll the dough out very thinly and evenly.

(11) Using a round cookie cutter, cut the thin dough into discs. They should be approximately 1½ inches in diameter (3.81 cm.). This should yield approximately 12 Cakes.

- (12) Using a flat-edged tool, impress an Egyptian Star ✶ on the top of each Cake.
- (13) Preheat the oven to 325° Farenheit.
- (14) Coat a flat baking pan with a thin layer of vegetable oil to prevent sticking.
- (15) Place the prepared Cakes, evenly spaced, upon the baking pan.
- (16) Bake the Cakes for 13–15 minutes at 325° Farenheit, watching them carefully throughout so they do not burn.
- (17) Remove from the oven and remove them from the cooking pan immediately. Place them upon a plate and allow the Cakes to cool to room temperature. Store them in an airtight, sanctified container in the Temple.

Milk and Honey

Ingredients:

1 Cup of whole Milk

Warm, pure Honey in the quantity desired.

Instructions:

(Prepare immediately before each Skry.)
- (1) Allow the milk to come to room temperature.
- (2) Gently warm the Honey until it is fluid.
- (3) Completely stir the Honey into the Milk.
- (4) Pour into the Cup sanctified for the Ritual and place it upon the Temple Altar.

Appendix VI

The Signs of Banishing and Invoking for the Pylons

Pylon One
Zemyeta
▽ of ▽

God Name
🐦𓌸𓀭 Geb[1]

BANISHING

INVOKING

Pylon Two
Sepedeta-wawau
△ of ▽

God Name
𓊪𓄿𓀭 Shu

BANISHING

INVOKING

Pylon Three
Nebeta-za-tzefu
▽ of ▽

God Name
𓏏𓆑𓏏 Tefnut[2]

BANISHING

INVOKING

---

[1] Pronounce "<u>Gob</u>-ee," with emphasis on the first syllable.

[2] Pronounce "<u>Tef</u>-ee-<u>nay</u>-ta," with emphasis on the first and third syllable.

Appendix Six

	BANISHING	INVOKING
PYLON FOUR *Eiry-ta* △ of ▽ God Name Sekhmet[3]		
PYLON FIVE *Nebeta-aḥau* ☽ God Name Khonsu		
PYLON SIX *Ḥemut-neb-es* ☿ God Name Anubis[4]		

---

[3] Pronounce "<u>Sakh</u>-may-ta" with emphasis on the first syllable.

[4] Pronounce "<u>An</u>-oo-pee" with emphasis on the first syllable. The "p" is hard, between a "p" and a "b."

The Visions of the Pylons

Pylon Seven
Pezedey-ta
♀

God Name
Ahathoor[5]

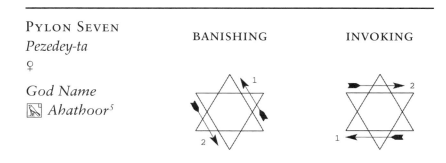

Pylon Eight: *Bekhekh-eya*

God Name: Asar-un-nefer[6]

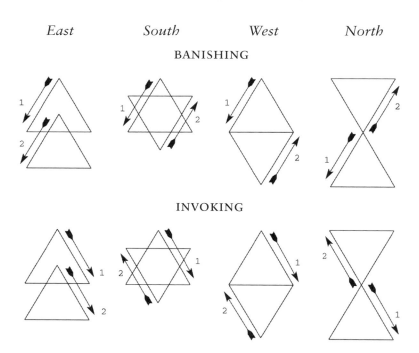

---

[5] Pronounce "Ah-ha-<u>toor</u>-ee," with emphasis on the third syllable.

[6] Pronounce "Ah-<u>sa</u>-ree-wen-<u>nof</u>-rah," with emphasis on the second and fifth syllable.

Pylon Nine: A'ata-shef-shefetu

⊙

God Name: ☌ Ra[7]

BANISHING

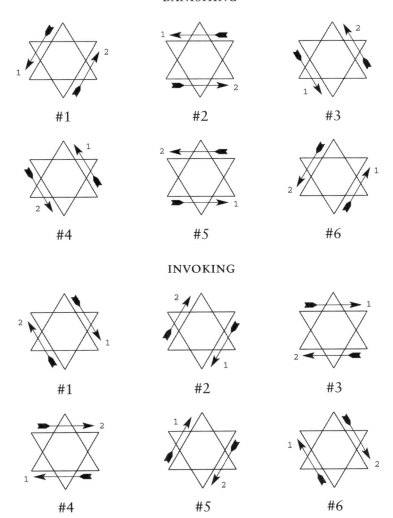

INVOKING

---

[7] Pronounce "Rah" (not Ray). The "r" in "Ra" should be trilled slightly.

Pylon Ten
Tzeserey-ta

♂

God Name

 Menthu[8]

BANISHING

INVOKING

Pylon Eleven
Sheta-besu

♃

God Name

 Amoun[9]

BANISHING

INVOKING

Pylon Twelve
Dezereta-bau

°°°
°°°

God Name

 Set[10]

BANISHING

INVOKING

---

[8] Pronounce "<u>Mon</u>-too," with emphasis on the first syllable.

[9] Prounounce "Ah-<u>moon</u>" with emphasis on the last syllable.

[10] Pronounce "<u>Set</u>-ee," with emphasis on the first syllable.

Bibliography

I. Published Editions by Aleister Crowley
(including *The Equinox*)

The Book of Lies which is also falsely called Breaks ... with an Additional Commentary to Each Chapter. Liber CCCXXXIII. Frater Perdurabo [pseud.]. Ilfracombe, 1962; rpt. New York: Weiser, 1972.

The Book of Thoth: A Short Essay on the Tarot of the Egyptians. The Master Therion [pseud.]. *Liber LXXVIII.* London, 1944; rpt. New York: Weiser, 1974.

The Collected Works of Aleister Crowley. 3 vols. London, 1905–07; rpt. Des Plaines, Ill.: Yogi Publication Society, n.d. [ca. 1973].

Commentaries to the Holy Books and Other Papers, ed. William Breeze. *The Equinox* IV(1). York Beach, Me.: Weiser, 1996.

The Confessions of Aleister Crowley: An Autohagiography, ed. John Symonds and Kenneth Grant. New York: Hill and Wang, 1969.

The Equinox. Vol. I, Nos. 1–10. London, 1909–13; rpt. New York: Samuel Weiser, 1974.

The Equinox. Vol. III, No. 1. Detroit, 1919; rpt. New York: Samuel Weiser, 1973.

The Equinox of the Gods. The Equinox III(3). London: O.T.O., 1936; rpt. New York: O.T.O./New Falcon Publications, 1991.

Liber Aleph vel CXI: The Book of Wisdom or Folly, ed. Karl Germer and Marcelo Motta. *The Equinox* III(6). West Point, Calif.: Thelema Publishing Co., 1961; 2d ed., ed. Hymenaeus Beta, York Beach, Me.: Samuel Weiser, 1991.

Little Essays Toward Truth. London: O.T.O., 1938; 2d ed., ed. Hymenaeus Beta, Scottsdale, Ariz.: New Falcon Publications, 1991. d

Magick (Book 4, Parts I–IV), ed. Hymenaeus Beta. 2d rev. ed., York Beach, Me.: Samuel Weiser, 1997.

Magick in Theory and Practice. London, 1929–30; rpt. New York: Dover Publications, 1976.

Magick without Tears, ed. Karl J. Germer. Hampton, N.J.: Thelema

Publishing Co., 1954; abridged 2d ed., ed. Israel Regardie, St. Paul: Llewellyn Publications, 1973.

The Tao Te Ching. Liber CLVII, trans. Aleister Crowley, ed. Hymenaeus Beta. *The Equinox* III(8). York Beach, Me.: Samuel Weiser, 1995.

ΘΕΛΗΜΑ: *The Holy Books of Thelema.* ed. Grady L. McMurtry and William Breeze. *The Equinox* III(9). York Beach, Me,: Weiser, 1983.

777 and other Qabalistic Writings, ed. Israel Regardie. New York: Weiser, 1986.

The Vision and The Voice with Commentary and Other Papers, ed. William Breeze. *The Equinox* IV(2). York Beach, Me.: Weiser, 1998.

II. General Works

Allen, James P. *Middle Egyptian.* Cambridge: Cambridge University Press, 2001.

Allen, Thomas George. *The Book of the Dead or Going Forth by Day.* Chicago: University of Chicago Press, 1974.

The Ancient Egyptian Coffin Texts, trans. R. O. Faulkner. 3 vols. Warminister: Aris and Phillips, 1973–78.

The Ancient Egyptian Pyramid Texts. trans. R. O. Faulkner. Oxford: Clarendon Press, 1969.

Avinoam (Grossman) Reuben. *Compendious Hebrew-English Dictionary*. Tel Aviv: Dvir Publishing Co. [no date].

Bauer, Walter. *A Greek-English Lexicon of the New Testament and other Early Christian Literature,* trans. William F. Arndt and F. Wilbur Gingrich. 2nd ed. rev. and augmented, Chicago: University of Chicago Press, 1979.

Berry, George Ricker. *Interlinear Greek-English New Testament.* Reading, Penn.: Baker Book House, 1981.

Betz, Hans Dieter. *The Greek Magical Papyri in Translation including the Demotic Spells.* Chicago: University of Chicago Press, 1986.

Birch, Samuel, ed. *Records of the Past, being English Translations of the Assyrian and Egyptian Monuments.* Vols. 10, 12. *Egyptian Texts.* London: Samuel Bagster and Sons, 1878, 1881.

Blavatsky, H. P. *Isis Unveiled: A Master Key to the Mysteries of Ancient and Modern Science and Theology.* 2 vols. New York: Theosophical Publishing Society, 1877.

———. *The Secret Doctrine: The Synthesis of Science, Religion and Philosophy.* 2 vols. New York: Theosophical Publishing Society, 1888.

Bonomi, Joseph and Samuel Sharpe. *The Alabaster Sarcophagus of Oimeneptah I, King of Egypt.* London: Longman, Green, Longman, Roberts and Green, 1864.

The Book of the Dead or Going Forth by Day, trans. Thomas George Allen. Chicago: University of Chicago Press, 1974.

The Book of Hades, trans. Eugene Lefébure; in Samuel Birch, ed., *Records of the Past,* Vols. 10, 12 (1878, 1881), q.v.

Browne, Henry. *Triglot Dictionary of Scriptural Representative Words in Hebrew, Greek and English.* New York: James Pott and Co., 1901.

Brugsch, Heinrich. *Religion und Mythologie der alten Aegypter.* 2 vols. Leipzig: J. C. Hinrichs, 1885.

Budge, E. A. Wallis: *An Account of the Sarcophagus of Seti I, King of Egypt, B.C. 1370.* London: British Museum, 1908.

———. *An Egyptian Hieroglyphic Dictionary.* 2 vols. London, 1920; rpt. New York: Dover Publications, Inc., 1978.

———. *The Egyptian Heaven and Hell. Books on Egypt and Chaldea,* Vols. 20–22. London: Kegan Paul, Trench, Trübner and Co., 1906.

———. *The Gods of the Egyptians; or Studies in Egyptian Mythology.* 2 vols. London: Methuen and Co., 1904.

———. *The Liturgy of Funerary Offerings.* London: Kegan Paul, Trench, Trübner and Co., 1909.

———. *Osiris and the Egyptian Resurrection.* 2 vols. London, 1911; rpt. New York: Dover Publications, Inc., 1973.

———. *A Vocabulary in Hieroglyphic to the Theban Rescension of the Book of the Dead.* London: Kegan Paul, Trench, Trübner and Co., 1898.

Campbell, Joseph. *The Masks of God.* 3 vols. New York: Penguin Books, 1979.

———. *The Mythic Image.* Princeton, N.J.: Princeton University Press, 1974.

Capel, Anne K. and Glenn Markoe. *Mistress of the House, Mistress of Heaven: Women in Ancient Egypt. New York: Hudson Hills in association with the Cincinnati Art Museum, 1996.

Case, Paul Foster. *The Tarot: A Key to the Wisdom of the Ages*. Los Angeles: Builders of the Adytum, 1990.

Černý, Jaroslav. *Coptic Etymological Dictionary*. London: Cambridge University Press, 1976.

Charles, R.H. *Apocrypha and Pseudepigrapha of the Old Testament*. 2 vols. Oxford: Oxford University Press, 1978.

Champollion, Jean-François. *Lettre à M. Dacier relative à l'alphabet des hiéroglyphes phonétiques*. Paris: Firmin-Didot Father and Son, 1822.

———. *Lettres écrites d'Égypte et de Nubie en 1828 et 1829*. Paris: Firmin-Didot Father and Son, 1833.

Coleman, Charles. *The Mythology of the Hindus*. London: Parbury, Allen and Co., 1832.

Cooper, W.R. *The Serpent Myths of Ancient Egypt*. London: Robert Hardwicke, 1873.

Crum, W.E. *A Coptic Dictionary*. London: Oxford University Press, 1979.

De Buck, Adriaan and Sir Alan H. Gardiner, eds. *The Egyptian Coffin Texts*. 7 vols. Chicago: University of Chicago Press, 1935–61.

Dickson, Paul. *Dictionary of Middle Egyptian in Gardiner Classification Order*. San Francisco: Internet Archive, 2006.

The Egyptian Book of the Dead: The Book of Going Forth by Day, being the Papyrus of Ani, trans. R.O. Faulkner and Ogden Goelet. San Francisco: Chronicle Books, 1994.

The Egyptian Book of Gates, trans. Erik Hornung. Zurich: Living Human Heritage Publications, 2014.

Erman, Adolf and Hermann Grapow. *Wörterbuch der Aegyptischen Sprache, im Auftrage der deutschen Akademien*. Leipzig and Berlin, 1926–63; rpt. Berlin: Akademie-Verlag, 1971.

Faulkner, Raymond O. *A Concise Dictionary of Middle Egyptian*. Oxford: Griffith Institute; Oxford University Press, 1962.

Frazer, James George, Sir. *Adonis, Attis, Osiris*. London and New York, 1906; rpt. New Hyde Park, N.Y.: University Books, 1961.

———. *The Golden Bough: A Study in Magic and Religion*. London and New York: Macmillan, 1960.

Gardiner, Alan, Sir. *Egyptian Grammar, being an Introduction to the Study of Hieroglyphs*. Oxford: Griffith Institute, 1957.

Gesenius' Hebrew-Chaldee Lexicon to the Old Testament Scriptures, trans. Samuel Prideaux Tregelles. Grand Rapids, Mich.: Baker Book House, 1979.

Gray, Louis Herbert, ed. *The Mythology of All Races*. Vol. I, *Greek and Roman*. Boston: Marshall Jones Co., 1916.

―――. *The Mythology of All Races*. Vol. XII, *Egyptian–Indo-Chinese*. Boston: Marshall Jones Co., 1918.

Gunther, J. Daniel. *The Angel and the Abyss, comprising The Angel and the Abyss and the Hieroglyphic Triad, Being Books II and III of The Inward Journey*. Lake Worth, Fla.: Ibis Press, 2014.

―――. *Initiation in the Æon of the Child, The Inward Journey*. Lake Worth, Fla.: Ibis Press, 2009.

Hall, Manly Palmer. *The Secret Teachings of All Ages*. Los Angeles: Philosopical Research Society, 1971.

Harding, M. Esther. *Woman's Mysteries Ancient and Modern: A Psychological Interpretation of the Feminine Principle as Portrayed in Myth, Story, and Dreams*. New York: Harper and Row, 1976.

Hennecke, Edgar. *New Testament Apocrypha*, ed. Wilhelm Schneemelcher. 2 vols. English trans., R. McL. Wilson. Philadelphia: Westminster Press, 1963.

Horner, George. *Pistis Sophia, Literally Translated from the Coptic*. London: Society for Promoting Christian Knowledge, 1924.

Hornung, Erik. *The Ancient Egyptian Books of the Afterlife*, trans. David Lorton. Ithaca, N.Y.: Cornell University Press, 1999.

The Holy Bible, containing the Old and New Testaments. Authorized Version, ed. C.I. Schofield. New York: Oxford University Press, 1945.

The Interlinear Bible Hebrew/English. 3 vols. trans. Jay P. Green, Sr. Grand Rapids, Mich.: Baker Book House, 1976.

Jacobi, Jolande. *Complex/Archetype/Symbol in the Psychology of C. G. Jung*, trans. Ralph Manheim. Princeton, N.J.: Princeton University Press, 1974.

Jellenik, Adolf. *Auswahl kabbalistischer Mystik. Heft I: Zum Theil nach Handschriften zu Paris und Hamburg, nebst historischen Untersuchungen und Charakteristiken*. Leipzig: A.M. Colditz, 1853.

Jéquier, Gustave. *Le Livre de ce qu'il y a dans L'Hades.* Abridged ed. Paris: Émile Bouillon, 1894.

Jung, Carl. *Aion: Researches into the Phenomenology of the Self,* trans. R. F. C. Hull. Princeton: Princeton University Press, 1978.

———. *Alchemical Studies,* trans. R. F. C. Hull. Princeton: Princeton University Press, 1976.

———. *Archetypes of the Collective Unconscious,* trans. R. F. C. Hull. Princeton: Princeton University Press, 1980.

———. *Man and His Symbols.* ed. New York: Dell Publishing, 1968.

———. *Memories, Dreams, Reflections,* trans. Clara Winston and Richard Winston. New York: Random House, 1965.

———. *Mysterium Coniunctionis,* trans. R. F. C. Hull, Princeton: Princeton University Press, 1976.

———. *Psychology and Alchemy,* trans. R. F. C. Hull, Princeton, NJ: Princeton University Press, 1977.

Lanzone, Ridolfo Vittorio. *Dizionario di Mitologia Egizia.* 3 vols. Turin, 1881–85; rpt. Amsterdam: J. Benjamins, 1974.

Lepsius, R. *Das Todtenbuch der Ägypter nach dem Hieroglyphischen Papyrus in Turin.* Leipzig, 1842; rpt. Osnabruck: Otto Zeller, 1969.

Lévi, Eliphas. *Transcendental Magic,* trans. A. E. Waite. London: George Redway, 1896.

Lichtheim, Miriam. *Ancient Egyptian Literature. Vol. II. The New Kingdom.* Los Angeles: University of California Press, 1976.

Liddell, George H. and Robert Scott. *A Greek-English Lexicon.* Oxford: Clarendon Press, 1968.

Lytton, Sir Edward Bulwer. *Zanoni.* London: Chapman and Hall, 1853.

Maspero, Gaston. *Les Hypogées Royaux de Thèbes,* in *Revue de l'Histoire des Religions,* Vol. 17. Paris: Ernest Leroux, 1888.

Mathers, S. L. *The Kabbalah Unveiled.* London, 1887; rpt. New York: Weiser, 1971.

Maystre, Charles and Alexandre Piankoff. *Le Livre des portes. Mémoires publiés par les membres de l'Institut français d'archéologie orientale du Caire,* Nos. 74, 75, 90. Cairo: L'Institut français d'archéologie orientale, 1939–62.

Mead, G. R. S. *Fragments of a Faith Forgotten.* New York: University Books, 1960.

———. *Pistis Sophia*. London: J. M. Watkins, 1921.

Mommsen, Theodore. *The History of Rome,* trans. William P. Dickson. 5 vols. New York: Charles Scribner, 1895.

Monier-Williams, Monier, Sir. *A Sanskrit English Dictionary*. Oxford, 1872; rpt. Delhi: Motilal Banarsidass, 2005.

Naville, Edouard. *Das Ægyptische Todtenbuch der XVIII bis XX Dynastie*. 3 vols. Berlin, 1886; rpt. Brighton: Elibron Classics, 2002.

Neumann, Erich. *Amor and Psyche: The Psychic Development of the Feminine. A Commentary on the Tale by Apuleius,* trans. Ralph Manheim. Princeton: Princeton University Press, 1973.

———. *The Great Mother: An Analysis of the Archetype*, trans. Ralph Manheim. Princeton: Princeton University Press, 1974.

———. *The Origins and History of Consciousness,* trans. R. F. C. Hull. Princeton: Princeton University Press, 1973.

Piankoff, Alexandre. *Mythological Papyri*. 2 vols. Bollingen Series 40. New York: Princeton University Press, 1957.

———. *The Shrines of Tut-Ankh-Amon*. Bollingen Series 40. New York: Princeton University Press, 1955.

———. *The Tomb of Rameses VI*. Bollingen Series 40/1. New York: Pantheon Books, 1954.

Pleyte, Willem. *Chapitres supplémentaires du Livre des Morts 162 à 174*. 3 vols. Leiden: E. J. Brill, 1881.

Rawlinson, George. *The History of Herodotus*. 4 vols. London: John Murray, 1862.

Regardie, Israel. *The Golden Dawn*. 4 vols. (in 2). St. Paul: Llewellyn, 1971.

Richardson, John and Francis Johnson. *A Dictionary of Persian, Arabic and English*. London: J. L. Cox, 1829.

Sand, Maurice and Alexandre Manceau. *Masques et bouffons (comédie italienne)*. 2 vols. Paris: Michel Lévy frères, 1860.

Sethe, Kurt. *Die Altaegyptischen Pyramidentexte nach den Papierabdrücken und Photographien des Berliner Museums*. Leipzig: J. C. Hinrich'sche Buchhandlung, 1908–10.

Sharpe, Samuel. *The Alabaster Sarcophagus of Oimenepthah I, King of Egypt*. London: Longman, Green, Longman, Roberts and Green, 1864.

Shennum, David. *English-Egyptian Index of Faulkner's Concise Dictionary of Middle Egyptian.* Malibu: Undena Publications, 1977.

Skeat, Walter W. *An Etymological Dictionary of the English Language.* New York: Macmillan and Co., 1882.

Spiegelberg, Wilhelm. *Koptisches Handwörterbuch.* Heidelberg: Carl Winters Universitätsbuchhandlung, 1921.

Stoll, Heinrich Wilhelm. *Handbook of the Religion and Mythology of the Greeks.* trans. R. B. Paul. London: Francis and John Rivington, 1852.

Sweizer, Andreas. *The Sun God's Journey through the Netherworld: Reading the Ancient Egyptian AmDuat.* Ithaca: Cornell University Press, 2010.

Takács, Gábor. *Etymological Dictionary of Egyptian.* 3 vols. Leiden: Brill, 1999, 2001, 2007.

Van der Molen, Rami. *A Hieroglyphic Dictionary of Egyptian Coffin Texts.* Leiden: Brill, 2000.

Vollmer, Wilhelm and Johannes Minckwitz. *Wörterbuch der Mythologie aller Völker*, ed. Wilhelm Binder. Stuttgart: Hoffmann, 1874.

Waite, Arthur Edward. *The Brotherhood of the Rosy Cross, being Records of the House of the Holy Spirit in its Inward and Outward History.* Secaucus, N.J.: University Books, 1973.

_____. *The Doctrine and Literature of the Kabalah.* London: Theosophical Publishing Society, 1886.

_____. *The Holy Kabbalah.* Secaucus, N.J.: University Books, 1960.

_____. *The Pictorial Key to the Tarot.* Secaucus, N.J.: University Books, 1966.

Westcott, W. Wynn. *The Chaldæan Oracles of Zoroaster,* ed. Sapere Aude (pseud. W. W. Westcott). *Collectanea Hermetica*, vol. VI. London: Theosophical Publishing Society, 1895.

Index

A∴A∴ 7, 8, 9, 10
A'ata-shef-shefetu 164, 185
ἅγιος 100
Abaddon 101
Abel 64
Abrahadabra 176
Abyss 10, 46, 49, 67, 82, 85, 89, 94, 101, 110, 112, 126
ACHHAShNV shiivl SHEETrI-FEE 36
Adam 120, 131
Adeptus Minor 105, 135
Adjuvo, Frater (Marcelo Ramos Motta) 21, 74
Adonai 43
Æon 38, 44, 46, 51, 62, 65, 117
    Lord of the 117
    New 51, 65
    of Isis 62
    of the Child 38, 65
    of the Father 62
    Old 51
    of Osiris 44, 46
Æthyr 21, 22, 23, 24, 52, 81
Age of Light 38
AHA 132, 133, 136
Ahathoor 175, 176, 184
Air (element) 43, 46, 52, 80, 85, 87, 89, 117
Aire 43, 44, 50, 51, 52, 55, 59, 60, 62, 66, 67, 74, 75, 86, 89, 90, 101, 113, 133
Akha-na-eiri 143, 150, 162
Akhenaten 15, 16
Alchemy 44
ALIM 52, 113, 120, 123
    Formula of 52, 120, 123
    Rite of 113

Alpha and Omega 112
Altar 55, 74, 77, 78, 117, 135, 172, 174, 175
Ambrosia 34
Amemut 73, 75
Amoun 186
Ancient of Ancient Ones 102
Angel 20, 22, 33, 34, 35, 47, 38, 43, 44, 45, 46, 48, 51, 52, 60, 62, 64, 65, 78, 80, 81, 82, 85, 86, 87, 88, 90, 91, 93, 95, 99, 100, 101, 104, 105, 109, 110, 111, 112, 113, 133, 135
    of Death 37
    Fallen 48
    Holy Guardian 20, 43, 80, 81, 135
Angelic 21, 24, 76
    Sigil of Fire 76
Ankh-af-na-Khonsu 176
Anubis 118, 120, 123, 183
Apollo 112
Apollyon 101
ARARITA 110
Archetypes 15, 19, 20
Archetypal 8, 60
Arik Anpin 102
Arjuna 109
Arrow 34, 52, 82, 91, 120, 123, 139
Āsana 82, 117, 175
    Dragon 117
Asar 118, 120
Asar-un-nefer 184
Ashvasena 109
Asi 94, 118
Assiah 50, 110
Astral 8, 23, 89, 117

Aten 16, 38
Atu 44, 51, 53, 59, 61, 73, 113, 123, 124, 129, 133, 134
    Atu I (The Magus) 61
    Atu II (The High Priestess) 73
    Atu III (The Empress) 129
    Atu VI (The Lovers) 113, 123, 124
    Atu IX (The Hermit) 59
    Atu X (Fortune) 133, 134
    Atu XVI (The Tower) 44, 51, 53
    Atu XX (The Aeon) 44
Aventine 123
Ba 14, 15, 88, 144
Babalon 71, 82
Babe of the Abyss 101
Balance 7, 9, 19, 20, 34, 75, 76, 103, 132
Banishing 19, 23, 89, 117, 143, 181, 182—186
Basilisk 102
Bast 48
Beast 34, 35, 37, 46, 72, 73
Bekhekh-eya 143, 163, 184
Bes-na-maut 176
Beth 60
Binah 34, 46, 65, 92, 126
Bird 14, 45, 46, 47, 60
Bitch of Damnation 48
Black 36, 46, 62, 76, 78, 91, 100, 101, 105, 111, 117, 118, 119, 126, 138, 139, 171
Blood 36, 37, 46, 52, 55, 62, 63, 65, 110, 123, 125
Blue 62, 89, 99
Book of Daniel, The 48
Book of Enoch, The 48
Book of Gates, The 14, 17, 18
Book of Genesis, The 48, 90, 123, 129
Book of Hades, The 17
Book of Job, The 126
Book of Jubilees, The 48
Book of Judges, The 63

Book of the Heart Girt with the Serpent, The 135
Book of the Heavenly Cow, The 13
Book of the Law, The 136
Book of Matthew, The 110
Book of Revelation, The 79, 101
Book of Thoth, The 63
Breath of Life 85, 131
Bride 34, 65, 102, 126, 135
Bridegroom 102, 135
Bull 60, 62, 74, 75
Bull-man 75
Burning coal 81
Burning face 143
Burning One 143
Burns with his eye 86, 142
C.R.C. 133
Caduceus 62, 63
Caelian 123
Cain 63, 64, 120, 123
Cake of Saffron 171, 172, 175, 177, 178
Camel 102
Cancer 43
Capita Mortua 44
Capitoline 123
Caput Draconis 126
Caput Mortuum 44
Case, Paul Foster 59
Castor and Pollux 108, 109
Cauda Draconis 126
Change = Stability 85
CHAOS 52
Chapel of Abominations 37
Charms of the snake 125
Chesed 64, 71, 101, 102, 111
Cheth 43, 133
Child 36, 38, 47, 48, 50, 51, 52, 63, 75, 77, 80, 91, 119, 120
    of Nu 36
    of Sorrow 52
    of the Moon 52
    of the Tower 51

Children 16, 51, 80, 109, 123,
    125, 138
    Of the Voice 123, 125
Chokmah 77, 78, 92, 109
Choronzon 90
Church 50
Circumambulator 144
City 38, 105, 110, 111, 118, 123,
    135, 139, 173
    of the Ibis 111
    of the Sun 38, 135, 139, 173
    upon the Seven Hills 123
Cleopatra 146
Cocatrice 35
Coiled One 142
Coils of the serpents 109
Construction 67, 111, 112
Corpses 44
Crab 131
Crone 34, 49
Crossroads 46
Crowley, Aleister 7, 8, 9, 63, 88,
    104, 110, 112, 113, 174
Crux Ansata 173, 174
Cube 89, 129
Cup 33, 34, 88, 111, 131, 132,
    172, 175
Daath 33, 37, 144
Dæmon 15, 50, 51, 125
Dais 71
Daughter 33, 34, 36, 74, 129
    of the Mighty Ones–129
Dead Head 44
Death 14, 15, 36, 37, 64, 100,
    132, 172
Deceptio visûs 46
Delphi 112
Δελφοι 112
δελφύς 112
Demon 37, 39
Destruction 9, 37, 44, 47, 51, 67
Devil 90, 102, 105
    Mighty 90
Dezereta-bau 144, 167, 186
Diana 91

Διόσκουροι 109
Diviners 125
Doer 142
Dog 89, 118, 120, 123
    in the Sun 120
Doorway 33, 100
Dove 132, 133
Dragon 33, 34, 37, 46, 52, 117,
    125
    Asana 117
    Breath of 33
    -Faced 47
Dragon-Beast-Queen 37
δράκων 125
Druids 43
Duant 13, 14, 15, 21, 29, 173,
    174, 175
Duat 13, 14, 15, 18
Dweller on the Threshold 101,
    102, 104
Earth 14, 18, 33, 44, 46, 51, 52,
    55, 62, 79, 80, 85, 86, 112, 119,
    123, 125, 143
ECCLESIASTIQUE SUMMAE 60
Ego 37, 48, 100, 112
Egypt 17
Egyptian 7, 8, 9, 10, 13–21, 24,
    38, 62, 73, 78, 94, 111, 118,
    132, 146, 173, 174
Eighty 81
Eiry-ta 69, 142, 159, 183
ἐγρήγοροι 48
Elements 21, 34, 43, 81
    Fire 21, 59, 62, 74, 76, 77,
        78, 80, 81
    Water 62, 91,
    Air 43, 46, 52, 80, 85, 87,
        89, 117
    Earth 33
    Water of 62
    Air of 46
Elohim 110, 129
ELOHIM TZABAOTH ARARI-
TA 110

Emperor 132
Empress 129
Empty One 99, 105
Enoch 123
    Book of, The 48
Enochian 25, 81, 104, 105, 118
Equilibrium 75
ἔργον 100
Esquiline 123
Eternal spinner 59
Eucharist 8, 171, 177
Europa 75
Eve 52, 120
Exempt Adept 24
Eye 9, 76, 81, 86, 93, 120, 133, 135, 139, 142, 143
    Eye of Hoor 120
    Eye of Horus 9
Father 52, 55, 62, 63, 74, 78, 123
    Dead 52, 120
    of the Voice 123
    Trinity of 65
    and Brother C.R.C. 133
Fire 59, 62, 74, 78, 80, 81
    and Flame 59
    of my Father 74
Firmament 90, 91, 174
First and the Last 112
Fishhook 126
Five Gods 81
Flame 59, 62, 75, 78, 79, 80, 99, 100, 135, 136, 142, 143
    Formless 79
    Living 75
    of the Vault 79
    Piercing 142
    Qadosh 62
    Secret 135
Flaming Child 80
Flaming Face 142
Flat bread 175
Fleur-de-lys 71
Foundation 20, 48, 85
Four of Wands 131

Formula of ALIM 120, 123
Furnace of desire 125
G∴D∴ 117
Gate 7, 14, 17, 18, 21, 33, 55, 59, 85, 99, 102, 105, 111, 129, 132, 133, 139, 144, 173
Gateway 21, 22, 39, 51, 59, 86
Geb 182
Geburah 21, 50, 52, 77, 78
Gemini 66, 109
Gernon, Richard (Gurney) 24, 25
Glossolalia 103
Glowing One 143
Goat 37, 75, 136
God 9, 10, 13, 14, 15, 16, 21, 36, 44, 50, 59, 60, 62, 65, 66, 76, 78, 80, 81, 88, 90, 91, 92, 93, 94, 95, 105, 110, 111, 113, 117, 118, 120, 123, 125, 129, 131, 172, 173, 174, 175, 182, 183, 184, 185, 186
    Dual 120
    Five 81
    Form 117, 175
    Golden 80
    House of 44
    Mighty 113, 123
    Monkey 120
    Moon 92, 94
    Name 13, 21, 50, 65, 110, 182, 183, 184, 185, 186
    of bloodshed 65
    of the moon 91, 94
    of magic and writing 91
    Slain 65
    smiling 93
    Son of 60
    Spirit of 129
    Sun 16
Goddess 8, 13, 34, 47, 64, 65, 71, 73, 75, 78, 86, 88, 89, 102, 126, 130, 133, 135, 136, 139
    of the Infinite Stars 78
    of the Moon 86

of the stars 47
of Witchcraft 34
ravaging 64
womb of 65
Gold 33, 80, 125
Golden 33, 71, 78, 80, 82, 101, 102, 135
    Desert 71
    Dawn 101
    God 80
    Lynx 102
    Raiment 78
    Red 78
    Rod 33
    Statue 135
    Sun 82
    Vial 78
Grade 8, 9, 24, 80, 135, 172
    of Adeptus Minor 135
    of Exempt Adept 24
    of Neophyte 80
Great of Respect 143
Great Sea 46, 126
Guardian 8, 9, 10, 17, 20, 23, 43, 80, 81, 82, 85, 99, 105, 112, 129, 130, 135, 141–153, 156–167
    of the Abyss 82
    of the Pylon 8, 17, 85
ἥλιος 100
Hades 17, 33
    Book of, The 17
Hadit 48, 49, 176
Hall of Truth 73
Halls of Love 131
Hammer of Thor 63, 67
Hanged Man 65
Hanged One 65
Hanging gardens 111
Hanuman 120
Hapax legomenon 126
Harlequin 58, 59
Harlot 81, 135
Harpies 46, 47

Hathor 10, 38, 75, 130, 133, 135, 136
He Who Utters 91, 109
He-She the queen 118, 125
Heart 9, 38, 73, 74, 75, 91, 100, 109
Heaven 44, 79, 133, 136
    Vault of 79
Hecate 46, 48, 49
Ḥemut-neb-es 107, 115, 142, 161, 183
Hermanubis 118, 120, 122
Hermaphrodite 65
Hermit 59, 64, 65
Herodotus 62
Heru 38
Heru-em-Anpu 120
Heru-ra-ha 117
Hexagram of Mercury 117
Hexagram 110, 117, 176
ϩⲓⲃⲱⲓ 111
High Priestess 73
Highest Assembly 60
Hippopotamus 73
Hod 21, 59, 62, 65, 66, 107, 110, 115
Holy Bridal Chamber 22
Holy Guardian Angel 20, 43, 80, 81, 135
Holy of Holies 101
Holy One 125, 135
Holy Order 71
Holy Spirit 129
Holy Word 418 132
ϩⲟⲙⲛⲧ 142
Honey 82, 171, 172, 175, 177, 178
Hoor 120, 123
Hoor-paar-kraat 103, 136
Horus 9, 10, 14, 15, 33, 38, 120
House of Darkness 173
House of God 44
House of the Hawk 131, 136
House of the Lesser Mother 62

House of the Sun 64
Huntress 91
Hut-Hooru 38, 75, 77
Hyacinth 135
I.A.T.A., Frater (Richard Gernon) 24, 25, 104, 117, 139
Iah 94
IAO 65, 118
ib (☥) 75
Ibis 60, 111
ΙΧΘΥΣ 60, 62
ιχθύς 60
ΙΕΡΟΣ 43
ΙΗΣΟΥΣ ΧΡΙΣΤΟΣ ΘΕΟΣ ΥΙΟΣ ΣΟΤΗΡ 60
Illusion of success 131, 132
Iniquity of the ages 85
Initiation 20, 37, 80, 101, 144
Initiation in the Æon of the Child 65, 79, 120
Invocation 23, 139
Invoking 110, 117, 172, 181, 182 183, 184 185, 185
IOI 103
ISU 94
Jasmine 135
Jawbone of an Ass 63, 64
Jesus 60, 110
JOY 102, 103, 133
Jubilees (Book of) 48
Judgment 9, 44, 126
Jung, C.G. 19, 20
Jungian 15 101
Jupiter 64, 71
JUSTICE 52, 74
K.N., Frater (J. Daniel Gunther) 67
ҚѦЈΝ 120
KAPH-PEH-ChETH 133
Karna Parva 109
Κάστωρ 109
Kether 102
Khabs 44
Khephra 176

Khonsu 93, 183
Khu 44
King 15, 65, 123, 125, 173
Kingdom 14, 16, 110, 125
ΚΛΕΟΠΑΤΡΑ 146
Knowledge 9, 20, 21, 37, 109, 125
Krishna 109
Kteis 43, 80, 89
Lady of Lifetime 142
Lady of the Sea 62
Lady of the Stars 85
Lambda 147
Law 7, 8, 13, 26, 66, 86, 91, 136
Lesser Countenance 102
Lesser Cup 33, 34
Lesser Sea 37
Leviathan 33, 34, 126
λήθιος 100
Liber 777 50, 112, 136
Liber A'ash 44, 119
Liber CCXX 74, 80, 85, 88, 113, 118, 125, 132, 136
Liber CCXXXI 113, 118
Liber DCCCXIII 46, 62
Liber LXV 13, 37, 46, 80, 81, 90, 101, 102, 103, 111, 119, 126, 135
Liber LXVI 126
Liber MCXXXIX 112
Liber O 23
Liber Tzaddi 37
Liber Viarvm Viæ 112
Liber VII 33, 43, 51, 80
Liber XVI 48
Lilith 119, 120, 121
Lingam 44
Living Flame 75
Lord of the Aeon 117
Lord of the Red Planet 52
Lovers 63, 123, 124, 125, 135
Lubber grasshopper (*Romalea Guttata*) 60
Lunar Crescent 43, 91

Index

Lynx 102
Maat 8, 71, 75, 90, 174
Macroprosopus 102
Magister Templi 34, 55, 67, 126
Magus 59, 60, 61, 78, 91, 104
Mahabharata 109
Maiden 49, 66
Malkah 34, 35, 102
Malkuth 21, 31, 33, 34, 35, 41, 50, 57, 59, 62, 65, 69, 74, 80, 102, 125
Manuscript 113
Master 46, 52, 59, 65, 118
   of Illusion 59, 65
   of the Earth 52
   of the Stone 59
   of the Temple 46, 118
Material Gain 131
Matter in motion 52
Matthew (N.T. Book of) 110
Māyā 59, 109
μαζουρωθ 126
Mazzaroth 126
Menthu 62, 63, 186
Mentu 176
Merchant 45, 46
Mercury 63, 66, 67, 92, 109, 117
Microprosopus 134, 102, 126
Mighty Devil 90
Milk 37, 171, 172, 175, 177, 178
Mistress of Nourishment 142
μνήμη 100
Monkey god 120
Moon 39, 43, 44, 46, 52, 55, 79, 86, 87, 89, 91, 92, 94
Motion 43, 44, 51, 52, 62, 85, 119, 129
Mountain 48, 51, 65, 80
Mountain of Abiegnus 65
Mouth of the Dead Father 52, 120
μόνον ιχθύν 60
Mudra 50
Mysteries of Creation 9, 80

Mysterious Initiation 144
Mystery of Air 85
Mystic Wheel 133
Nadis 22
NAKHEShT 43, 55
Navel of the Earth 112
Nebeta-aḥau 97, 142, 160, 183
Nebeta-za-tzefu 57, 142, 158, 182
Neferu-Ha-Neter 38
Nemo 126
Neophyte 34, 37, 80, 117
Nephilim 48
Nephthi 118
Netzach 21, 65, 71, 75, 77, 78, 127, 132
New Aeon 51, 65
Nine of Pentacles 131
No Man 67, 80, 126
Nod 123
NOX 43, 48
NOX-ה-𒈬 43
Nu 36, 174
Nuit 48, 78, 85, 176
O madâ-i 81
O go go madâ-a anatahèretzâ ... 81
Oath 36, 37, 38, 87, 99, 113, 117
ODO QO KI KIKALE 118
ὀμφαλός 112
Old Aeon 51
ON 135, 139, 173
One fish 60
OOϱ 94
OOHA 94
Oracle 35, 36, 112, 113, 123
Oracle of the Mighty Gods 113, 123
Orange 62, 117, 118, 126
Order 7, 9, 67, 71, 88, 101
Orifice 33
Osiris 13, 14, 33, 44, 46, 173
Outer College 8, 9, 67, 139
Outer Order 67
Palace 64, 78, 80, 82, 90, 109

Palatine 123
Pantacle 113, 116, 117, 171, 172, 175, 176
Paradoxia 19, 33, 34, 35, 37
Passover 37
Pastos 133
Path (of the Tree of Life) 21, 22, 65, 136, 139
Pearl 45, 46
Peh 44, 52, 123, 133
Pekhereya 144, 153, 167
Pentagram of Air 89, 117
PERFECTION 118, 131
Pezedey-ta 127, 143, 162, 184
ΦΑΛΛΟΣ 51, 89, 91
Phallus 33, 37
Phantasmagoria 46
Philistines 64
Philosophus 9, 76, 129, 133
Phineas 46
Piercing Flame 142
Pillars of the Universe 59
Point 48, 52, 85, 102
Πολυδεύκης 109
Portal 125, 135
Priestess 38, 73, 112
Prophet 7, 51, 52, 176
πυθία 112
Pylon 8, 9, 10, 13-19, 21-25, 31, 36-39, 43, 44, 49-52, 59, 60, 65, 71, 75, 76, 85, 86, 87, 99, 109, 110-113, 117, 129, 139, 141-145, 147, 148, 149-153, 156-167, 169, 171, 181-186
Pythia 112
Python 102, 112
Pythoness 112, 113
Qab-eya 142, 148, 157
Qadosh 62
θάνατος 100
θελημα 37, 71, 100
Qliphoth 46, 47, 101
Queen 34, 35, 37, 48, 62, 65, 102, 113, 118, 125, 129
QUEShEMANAMAH 50

Quirinal 123
Ra 13, 14, 173, 176, 185
Ra-Hoor-Khuit 138, 176
Ram 14, 15, 131,
Rashith Ha Gilgalim 85
Redemption 44, 55
Remethu 15
Reni reni gaga... 103
Revelation (N.T. Book of) 79, 101
Rite of ALIM 113
Rite of H 113
Ritual 19, 62, 171
Rome 123
Romulus and Remus 123
Rose 48, 64, 111, 126, 135
Rosy Cross 117
Ruach 35, 65, 67, 99, 100, 111, 129
Ruach Elohim 129
Sabeya 144, 153, 167
Sacred Harlot 135
Sacred Souls 144
Sacrificial stone 76
Saffron 171, 172, 175, 177, 178
Samādhi 22, 82
Saṃsāra 33
Samson 64
Sanctified One 143
Sanctuary 43, 86, 90 102, 109, 135
Sanctuary of the Lady 86
Satan 110
Satyr 37, 102
Scales 129
Scorpion 132, 139
Scribe 10, 24, 25, 87, 101, 103, 104, 113, 117, 139, 171, 172, 173, 175, 176
Seal 71, 104, 155
Seaman 45, 46
Seeing one 125
Seeker 10, 74
Seer 9, 10, 101, 171, 172, 173, 174, 175, 176
Sekhmet 48, 183

Selah 82
Selene 86
ΣΕΛΗΝΗ 86
Sepedeta-Wauwau 41, 142, 157, 182
Sephira 21, 59, 91, 130
Sephiroth 21, 23, 65, 80, 102, 111, 123, 130
Serpent 10, 34, 59, 74, 85, 109, 112, 119, 120, 132, 142, 143, 144, 145
  of the Staff 59
  of the Tree 74
  -One 85
  Uraeus 10
Set 13, 36, 102, 103, 186
Seta-ma-eiri-fa 86, 142, 149, 160
Sethu 143, 152, 165
Sety I 10, 16, 17, 18
Seven Hills 123, 125
Seven of Cups 132
Shaddai El-Chai 50
Shekinah 43
Shells 46, 73, 101
Sheta-besu 144, 166, 186
Shining One 143
Shrine 38, 136
Shu 85, 95, 99, 182
Shut of eye, 143
Sigil 8, 76, 113, 116, 118, 145, 146, 147
Sigil of Zooωasar 113, 116, 118
Sign 66, 81, 84, 85, 95, 99, 103, 109, 118, 126, 129, 172, 173, 174, 181,
  of Adoration 172, 173
  of Attack 172, 173
  of Banishing 181
  of Crux Ansata 173, 174
  of Defense 172, 173
  of Gemini 109
  of Hoor-paar-kraat 103
  of Invoking 172, 181
  of Mercury 66
  of Shu 84, 85, 95, 99

  of Silence 173
  of Passing 85
  of the Enterer 173
  of the Philosophus 129
  of the Zodiac 126
  of Venus 81
Silence 44, 51, 65, 71, 73, 99, 101, 104, 105, 173
Sistrum 130
Skeleton 93
Skry 97, 115, 139, 169, 171
Smooth Point 102
Snake 109, 125, 176
Son 14, 52, 60, 85, 86, 102, 109
  of Earth 85
  of God 60
  of the Ancient of Ancient Ones 102
Sorrow 48, 52, 54, 80
Spacetime 22, 59
Speech 16, 19, 21, 44, 48, 87, 91, 100, 132, 176
Sphere 50, 59, 99, 130
Sphinx 34, 111
Spider 59
Spirit of God 129
Spittle 34, 112, 125
Squaring the Circle 89
Staff of Construction 67
Star 9, 44, 47, 51, 67, 78,7 9, 85, 89, 126, 139,1 76,
Star Wormwood 79
Starry Abode 7, 13, 16, 29, 174, 175
Steals with his eye 143
Stélé of revealing 77, 88
Sterility 46, 55
Stinging One 142
Stink of Roses 126
Stone 37, 38, 43, 44, 45, 46, 50, 51, 52, 55, 59, 71, 76, 78, 79, 80, 85, 87, 99, 100, 111, 146
  Rosetta 146
  Shew- 50, 99
Stylus of the divine 125

Sun 7, 14, 15, 16, 38, 43, 44, 52, 64, 66, 82, 87, 100, 120, 132, 135, 139, 173
Supreme Chiefs 60
Sword 52, 54, 71, 72, 74, 75, 86, 88, 102, 105, 110, 117, 118
   Ace of 71, 72
   hidden 88
   of Justice 74
   of Zaur Anpin 102
   Three of 52, 54
Ta-Nech 176
Tahuti 78, 91, 92, 94, 109, 111, 175
Talisman of its Lord 142
Tao Te Ching 104
TAR, नृ 143
TARA, तर 143
Tarot 24, 45, 53, 54, 59, 61, 71, 72, 92, 93, 124, 133, 134
Tarot Cards
   Ace of Swords 71, 72
   Death 132
   Fortune (The Wheel) 133, 134
   Four of Wands 131
   Nine of Pentacles 131
   Seven of Cups 132
   The Emperor 132
   The Empress 129
   The Hanged Man 65
   The Hermit 59, 64, 65
   The Lovers (or Brothers) 123, 124
   The Magus 61
   The Priestess 73
   The Star 126
   The Tower 51, 52, 53
   The Universe 93, 132
   Three of Swords 52, 54
   Two of Cups 111, 131
Tefnut 182
Teka-hor 142, 149, 159
τελεσμα 142
τελεσμός 142
τελέειν 142
τέλος 142
Temple 46, 51, 55, 62, 101, 117, 118, 172, 176
   of Menthu 62
Terrible One 105
The Desert 46, 142
The Egyptian Heaven and Hell 17
Thelema 7, 8, 37, 38, 88, 133
Third Order 67
Thoth 9, 65, 91, 173
Thoth Tarot 24, 53, 54, 61, 72, 124, 133, 134
Throne 48, 71, 73, 75, 78
Tilsam طلسم 142
Tiphereth 22, 65, 91, 102, 135, 139
Tomb 8, 10, 15, 16, 77, 90, 100, 102
Top of the Earth 143
Tower 51
Tree 74, 80
Tree of Life 21, 22, 80, 81
Tribulations 33
Tripod 100, 112, 113
Trump 45
Truth 9, 50, 73, 85, 87, 90, 102, 111, 112
Tuat 13
Tum 176
Twelve Banners of the Name 136
Twins 66, 109, 123
Tzaddi 37, 126
Tzedebeya 142, 148, 158
Tzeserey-ta 143, 165, 186
Unconscious 14, 15, 19, 20, 37, 47, 60, 73, 79
Underworld 15
Upward Arrow 119, 120
Urns 71
Utterance of the Pythoness 112, 113
V.I.T.R.I.O.L. 125

VAHYEH 136
Vast Countenance 102
Vau 66
Vault 79, 85
Veil 10, 35, 48, 59, 79, 118
Venom 112, 125
Venus 80, 81, 135
Vesica Piscis 85, 99
Vial 74, 78
VIAOV 65, 66
Viminal 123
Virgin 33, 91, 102, 103, 131, 135
   of Eternity 135
Vision 7, 8, 9, 13, 19, 20, 21, 22, 23, 24, 35, 36, 44, 48, 50, 55, 59, 63, 65, 71, 73, 75, 80, 82, 86, 88, 95, 101, 104, 105, 109, 110, 113, 117, 123, 126, 129, 130, 132, 133, 135, 138, 176
   of Beauty 65
Vision and the Voice, The 9
Visita Interiora Terrae Rectificando Invenies Occultum Lapidem 125
Voice 29, 33, 51, 59, 75, 78, 80, 89, 90, 93, 100, 102, 111, 118, 119, 123, 125, 126, 129, 133, 135, 136, 138, 139, 175
   Children of the 123, 125
   of Fire 78
Warlord 52, 65
Warriors 125
Watcher 48, 49

Water 14, 34, 36, 37, 46, 55, 60, 65, 74, 78, 79, 86, 90, 91, 103, 104, 111, 113, 129
Wepet-ta 143, 147, 151, 164
Western Desert 142
Wheel 133
Whirling First Motion 85
Will, The 19, 26, 39, 51, 86
Wine-bibbing 125
Wisdom and Knowledge 125
Within his poison 144
Wolf 123
Womb 52, 65, 78, 91, 112
Worm holes 21
Wormwood 78, 79
Yellow Cape 117
Yemy-netu-fa 144, 147, 152, 166
Yesod 21, 43, 44, 46, 49, 50, 51, 52, 83, 85, 91, 97, 101, 102, 111
Yethy-ma-eiri-fa 143, 150, 161
Yod 59, 62, 82, 90, 123
Yoni 44
Zanoni 101
Zau Zemyeta 142, 147, 156
Zauir Anpin 102
Zayin 126
Zemyeta 31, 142, 156, 182
Zeta-hor 143, 151, 163
Zeus 75, 109
Zodiac 43, 109, 126
Zohar, The 102, 125
Zooωasar 113, 116, 118

Initiation in the Æon of the Child
Book I of The Inward Journey
J. Daniel Gunther

In 1904, *The Book of the Law (Liber AL vel Legis)* declared the advent of a new period in the course of human history—the Æon of Horus or Æon of the Child. The doctrine codified in the *Book of the Law,* and numerous other Holy Books, is known as *Thelema* (a Greek word meaning "Will"). Aleister Crowley was revealed as the Prophet of the New Æon.

In this ground-breaking book, author J. Daniel Gunther provides a penetrating and cohesive analysis of the spiritual doctrine underlying and informing the Æon of the Child, and the sublime formulas of Initiation encountered by those who would probe its Mysteries. Drawing on more than thirty years of direct experience as a student and teacher within the Order of the A∴A∴, the author examines the doctrinal thread of Thelema in its historical, religious and practical context. He also provides detailed discussions and expositions of many of the cryptic passages within the Holy Books of Thelema.

Much of Thelemic doctrine is presented here for the first time in clear, precise language that will aid those students who seek to navigate the difficult terrain of the Spiritual quest. More advanced students will find tantalizing clues to serve as guideposts and eventual confirmation of direct experience.

With numerous diagrams and detailed references encompassing ancient Egyptian hieroglyphic texts, the Apocrypha, the Old and New Testaments, Alchemy, Hermetic Qabalah, and Tarot, as well as Carl Jung and Aleister Crowley.

ISBN: 978-0-89254-209-3
224 pages, 6" x 9". • Now in Paperback • $24.95

The Angel & The Abyss
Books II & III of The Inward Journey
J. Daniel Gunther

In this companion to *Initiation in the Æon of the Child*, author J. Daniel Gunther provides detailed and cohesive analysis of the two major spiritual crises in the career of the aspirant in the Æon of the Child—the Knowledge & Conversation of the Holy Guardian Angel and the Crossing the Abyss between the divine realms and the human. Expounding on the sublime Formulas of Initiation confronting those who would aspire to these Mysteries, the author draws deeply from Jungian psychology, world mythology and religion, and the doctrines of the classic Mystery traditions, explaining how the revelations of Thelema apply to the individual.

In 1904, *The Book of the Law* declared the advent of a new period in the course of human history—the Æon of Horus or Æon of the Child. The doctrine codified in *The Book of the Law*, and numerous other Holy Books, is known as Thelema (a Greek word meaning "Will"). Aleister Crowley was revealed as the Prophet of the New Aeon.

The Angel & The Abyss is written in clear, precise language that will aid those students who seek to navigate the difficult terrain of this advanced stage of the Spiritual quest. More knowledgable students will find tantalizing clues to serve as guideposts and eventual confirmations of their direct experience.

With numerous diagrams, this volume is copiously illustrated in both black & white and color.

ISBN: 978-0-89254-211-6
400 pages • 6" x 9" • $40.00

About the Author

J. Daniel Gunther is a life-long student of esotericism, mythology and religion. For over forty years he has been a member of A∴A∴, the teaching Order established by Aleister Crowley. He is considered one of the foremost authorities on the doctrines of Thelema and the syncretic method of Magick and Mysticism taught by A∴A∴. He is on the editorial board of *The Equinox*, published by Weiser, and has served as consultant and advisor for numerous other publications in the field of occultism. He is the co-editor of the definitive Ibis Press edition of Thomas Stanley's *Pythagoras: His Life and Teachings*. Gunther is an Egyptological scholar whose most recent contribution has been featured in the twentieth anniversary edition of *The Egyptian Book of the Dead: The Book of Going Forth by Day* published by Chronicle Books.

www.jdanielgunther.com

Parties interested in contacting A∴A∴
may address their correspondence to:

Chancellor
BM ANKH
London WC1N 3XX
England
email: secretary@outercol.org